Welcome to the 2022 edition of Buying in Italy, now in its 12th edition. The aim of this book is to help people who are looking to buy a property in Italy over the next two years or so, and we have decided to issue a newly revised edition with all the recent updates to the law. The new government is introducing new laws almost weekly, so it is very important to have a guide which is regularly updated. Undoubtedly things will change again over the next 12 months, and that is why we offer free updates to the book.

To receive the free updates you will need to let us know at Buying in Italy. Send an email together with proof of purchase – (a screenshot of your paypal payment is fine) and we will add you to the updates mailing list. Be sure that updates@buyinginitaly.com is on your allowed list. You will not receive any other email from this address, other than your regular updates.

The 'B' word

So, finally, we have it. What will Brexit mean for those of you who want to buy a property in Sicily? As far as the actual purchase goes, absolutely nothing changes. If you plan to rent it out and/or use it for holidays, then nothing has changed.

If, on the other hand, your grand design involves driving to and from the UK with your labradoodle, getting Italian residency and possibly a job using your UK accountancy qualification, then things are going to be more difficult than they were between 1975 and 2020.

Individual stumbling blocks are covered in the relevant sections of what follows. If you want to go straight to the relevant sections, here are some links:

Cars and Driving

Banking

Residency

The 'C' Word

Covid 19 has changed all our lives. Apart from it being more difficult to get to your place in the sun, the pandemic hasn't actually affected the process of buying and living in Italy. Certain things have been frozen in time and prorogued, but by the time you are reading this the effects will be few and far between.

Travel has been the main problem over the last two years. Whether it's Air Italy going bust, Ryanair cancelling routes willy nilly, the need to book an entire compartment on the train for one person or car hire rates going through the roof, Covid has make us all think about the wisdom of buying a place in a place you can't actually get to. Homeowners, though, are extremely resilient, and as we get used to the new rules for travelling, things will assume a new normality. The idea of a couple of months by a crystal blue sea outweighs the inconvenience of wearing a mask for a couple of hours.

INDEX

Why me?

PART ONE - Looking

Why Italy?

Estate Agents

I've got two days to find my dream home....

Buying to Let

Renting

PART TWO – Buying

Paperwork

    Codice Fiscale

    Visure –   Catastale

                        Ipotecarie

    Destinazione Urbanistica

    Conformita Urbanistica

    Proposta di Aquisto

    Compromesso Transcription

    Act of Rogito   Prelazione

<u>Underdeclaration</u>

<u>Prima Casa</u>

Buying to Restore

Buying to Build

Buying Off plan

Insurance

Swimming Pools

PART THREE – Living

Utilities

       Electricity , Gas, Heating, Water, Telephone, Television

Banks

Post Office

Cars and Driving

Car Insurance

Local Taxes

       TARI, IMU & TASI, Water, Canone Rai

Health

Education

Holidays

Earning a Living

Making a Will

Moving

Appendices

Glossaries

Catastal Classifications

Luxury property

Residence

Notaios costs

Architects fees

Links

Why me?

It's now twelve years since I first published this book, and it affords me not a little smugness that a ferry load of people has used the information herein to help them buy a property in Italy. A lot has changed in the property market since I first put pixel to screen, and in many ways the situation has improved immeasurably for foreign buyers. In fact, it is now so complicated to buy a property that many of the 'blokes at the bar' who previously offered to help you, have now given up. In their place is an army of geometras, architects and the like who have decided that they can offer their expertise with a straight face and get their clients to buy a house which will let said geometra buy a Porsche within a year. Of course now more people have bought homes in Italy, there are more potential buyers who have a friend who is an expert because they've already bought a flat in Florence. I spend quite alot of my time sorting out the resulting mess.

I'm an estate agent, the only qualified, registered and legally operating English estate agent in Sicily. I did the course, sat the exams and learned an inordinate amount of useless information that I will never use in my job. Sitting at a long table facing 4 professionals in my oral exam the question was how would I calculate the worth of a pile of manure if I were selling a farm. They wanted a pithy response which I still don't know, what they got was a lengthy diatribe in not very good Italian about whether an estate agent needs to know the nitrogen content of cow crap. However, I passed the exams, and from that point on have learned a seemly amount of facts about buying and selling property in Italy. The trouble is we're in Italy, and the facts change with the weather, which is why I thought it would be a rippingly good idea to provide free updates – the internet is good for some things besides short films of domestic animals behaving in a mildly amusing manner.

Of course this alone doesn't mean the book will be any good – but I was a writer (or rather, like an alcoholic, – I am a writer, but I'm just not writing today), so hope the facts will be strung together in a readable way. Of course I would like you to buy through my agency, but should you decide to buy using someone else's services, I'd like you to do it in an informed way. The power of the internet is such that you can ruin someone's reputation with a well phrased line in a blog – and there are plenty of agents and non agents here in Italy that deserve it. I hope I will never be one of them, which is why I've tried to provide the basics and, hopefully, let you see that it's not always the estate agent's fault if something doesn't go to plan.

Enjoy the book, buy a house and enjoy Italy – it's worth the effort.

Ramsay Gilderdale

Part One

Looking

Why Italy?

Estate Agents

I've got two days to find my dream home....

Buying to Let

Renting

Why Italy?

Italy isn't for everyone. If you are looking for a little England – a vibrant expat scene, lots of people who speak English, panto, cricket, and the ability to buy a Daily Telegraph without driving 50 miles – then perhaps Italy isn't for you, and certainly not the south. It's not a country to emigrate to if you just want sun. You have to be in love with the country, the culture and the people. You cannot properly live in Italy by segregating yourself – you will never be happy. If you want to be here, embrace the whole concept and you will live contentedly, if you don't let yourself become the slave of bureaucracy! If you feel that you cannot live without other English speakers around, you'd be better off staying north of Rome, though Puglia does have a vibrant expat community now. Bear in mind that just because you want to discuss the last tango on Strictly, and the latest plot lines of the Archers doesn't necessarily mean that the nearest native English speaker will want to do the same. As I said, most people come here to immerse themselves in Italian life, and not all want to be reminded of what they left behind so willingly.

How many tourists have been in Florence in a day, whizzed round the Forum in Rome and then gone home claiming to have 'done' Italy? To 'do' Italy justice would take a lifetime. I have walked the length and breadth of Tuscany, know Umbria well, been to Rome, passed many months in Puglia and

Basilicata, lived in Naples and now reside in Sicily, holidayed in every region bar Aosta, and I cannot claim to know my adopted homeland. Italy is big. And long. What I have discovered is that it takes an epic desire to travel to go from Sicily to Milan, and I prefer everything south of Rome. You can take north of Bologna and put it where you will, it doesn't interest me, other than the 'once in a lifetime' visit to Venice. Sitting down with a map and deciding you want to live right <u>there</u>, won't help matters. Most people who decide to make Italy their home usually arrive at their final destination by trial and error, or by supremely happy circumstance.

Most peoples' first taste of Italy is a long weekend in 'the eternal city', the 'Serenissima' or a week's summer hols in Tuscany. And why not? You have to start somewhere. Watching the palio in Siena, however, won't give you a fundamental understanding of the Catanian feast of Sant'Agata – the thing to remember is that as Metternich so profoundly said – Italy is not a country, its a geographical expression. Unified for only 160 years, Italy is a collection of smaller countries which have the same TV stations.

Italy is divided in to 20 regions, of which 5 are semi autonomous with some of their own laws. These are the two big islands, Sardinia and Sicily, and 3 of the regions at the tippety north - Aosta, Fruili Venezia Giulia and Trentino Alto Adige.   The final three are good for skiing and cross border activities. Sicily and Sardinia have lots of sea and sun.

The 20 regions are subdivided into provinces which are administrative areas, each with a provincial capital and responsibility for local planning, police and fire brigades, and transport. In all there are 110 provinces – Lombardy with the most, and Aosta with the least, - none – in that the region is the province. In 2016 Matteo Renzi abolished the provinces, which 6 years on are still alive and well and living under assumed names. So now you understand why some Italian towns have terrible roads and planning problems while the town next door is virtually impeccable, we can go through them one by one.

ABRUZZO – in the middle next to Lazio. Newly 'discovered' for its cheap housing and low cost flights, Abruzzo also had a severe earthquake in April 2009 when the provincial capital of Aquila was hit by an earthquake which counted over 300 dead. The people who buy in Abruzzo are fanatically loyal to their region, it has natural parks, uncontaminated coastlines and skiing in the winter. It is also years behind other spots in Italy and is included in the 'south' of the country as far as its infrastructure is concerned.

AOSTA – the smallest region it has only 130.000 or so inhabitants. Up in the top left, it is nearly all Alp. Go, ski and eat fondue.

APULIA – the posh name for Puglia, it's the longest region in Italy and covers 400 Km from north to south. It's the heel of the country, host to beautiful towns such as Lecce and Alberobello and others such as Taranto. Firmly a region of the 'mezzogiorno' it has its own 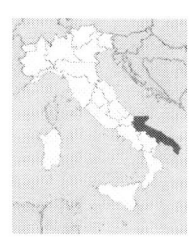 organised crime outfit, the SCU or the Sacra Corona Unita and a dire transport system. It has some of the best beaches in Italy, and a thriving Expat population who have bought trulli – the little Tolkienesque stone built houses – and restored them into bed and breakfasts. The Salento – the south of the province, is flat- very flat, and is ideal for bicyclists and people who don't worry that the rise in sea levels will obliterate the lowest lying parts of Italy within a generation. Madonna visits and Helen Mirren owns, but it's shut in winter and increasingly gets snow.

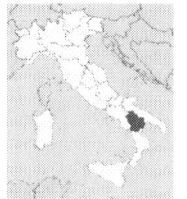 BASILICATA – next to Puglia, is the instep of the Italian boot, and if you want to live in a spot which hasn't changed in the last 100 years, then Basilicata's your place. Newly popular thanks to Mel Gibson – the town of Matera has rediscovered cave dwelling, (as in truth has all of southern Italy and Sicily), and now has chic expensive hotels and is a must see stop on the tourist trail.

CALABRIA – should be the most beautiful place in Europe. But the 'Ndrangeta – the Calabrian mafia, and a complete lack of

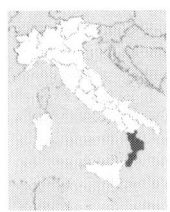
interest by government have made sure that its been comprehensively sullied in the last 40 years. It has bright spots undoubtedly, but the lure of easy money and weak cement has made Calabria top of the list as far as home buyers horror stories go.

CAMPANIA – It should be the flower of Italy, it has history, culture, cuisine – but also the Camorra, which has eaten it from inside out. Naples, one of the most fascinating cities in Europe, has been in thrall to organised crime for generations and doesn't wear it well. Despite having the Amalfi coast, Capri, Paestum and lots of other breathtaking bits of scenery, it also has a large, unpredictable volcano.

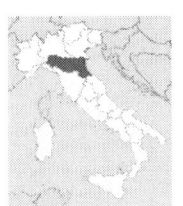
EMILIA ROMAGNA – big, chic and wealthy, the birthplace of Mussolini, and home to Bologna, Rimini and Parma – high standard of living and jobs. Oh, and fog. Lots of fog.

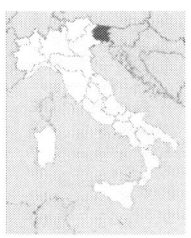
FRIULI VENEZIA GIULIA – autonomous part of Italy that was for a long time part of Austria. If you like your Italian with a Austrian flavour, Trieste and lots of immigrants from over the border, it's heaven.

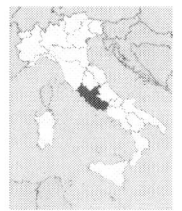

LAZIO - two football teams and a Pope. Home of the Etruscans, and host to the capital city, Lazio is worth exploring – to the north the volcanic lakes, to the south the reclaimed mosquito infested Pontine marshes with fascist era 'new towns' such as Latina and mountains to the east.

LIGURIA – small and perfectly formed it takes up the crescent shaped coast of the north west, and hogs all the best beaches from its northerly neighbours. Genova, La Spezia, Portofino – its all rather nice and with a superb climate, except for when it rains. Which it does. Alot.

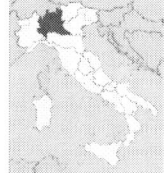

LOMBARDIA – or greater Milan as it is becoming. Gold, furs and lots of money abound. Reputedly the most racist region, as well as the most populated with nearly 1/5th of all Italy's population.

LE MARCHE - It started out as the poor man's Tuscany, after Umbria shook off the mantle and became rather well to do. It has coastline, mountains and nice bits inbetween, as well as the cities of Urbino and Ascoli Piceno. The English love it, at least for 5 or 10 years and then think about moving on.

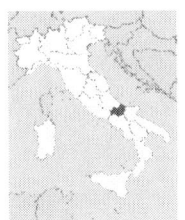
Severe earthquakes in 2016 have created problems for many comunes.

MOLISE – the second smallest, mountainous, and the latest stamping ground for intrepid low cost home seekers.

PIEMONTE - surrounded on 3 sides by Alps and at the head of the Po Valley. Torino is a happy city, except for the smog.

SARDEGNA – Easy to get to, blessed with incredible seas and wealthy tourists. Inland is best left to the Sards. The east coast is where it's at, but the south (Cagliari) is not to be snubbed.

SICILIA – a paradise on earth if it had politicians that were worth their salt. Stunningly beautiful, fertile and home to incredible coastlines, breathtaking countryside, fabulous food, wonderful wines – am I too partial? Historical home of the Mafia and a country that culturally lives in the past. A melting pot of European and African cultures, with a bit of ancient Greece thrown in. The

Sicilians like to build in cement, lots of cement, so don't expect an aspic covered days of yore experience.

TRENTINO ALTO ADIGE– Ski. Speak other languages. Summer lasts a week.

TOSCANA – There's nothing left to say. It has Florence, San Gimignano, and Siena. It's beautiful, expensive, and full of tourists.

UMBRIA – Smaller hillier version of Tuscany. No coastline, lots of wild boar, and lately prone to seismic activity

VENEZIA – More to it than Venice – Vicenza, Verona, Padova are all nice, if fog bound cities. 57% of the region is in the Po Valley, the rest is mountains. Industrial and rich.

That's it as far as a guide to Italy goes. I assume that by the time you have decided to buy in Italy, you have taken the time and trouble to find out where it is, what it looks like and how you can get here. It would, in fact, be too easy reproducing the Wikipedia on Italy, its regions, its provinces and interesting statistics on the quality of life. That is not why I expect you are buying this book. So let's just leave it at that and say no more. If you don't know where you want to buy, do some research or hop on a plane. So, that's saved 100 pages and we can get down to the gritty reality of property purchases.

Italy is, now unified for 160 years, a country. However, as in other countries it can be useful to draw some theoretical internal borders – at least for generic sweeping statements that will annoy some readers.

The North, The Middle and The South. Let's jump on that bandwagon.

For the purposes of this book the north shall be the Green Padania bit at the top, the 'red' south and Sardinia, and the white central part of Emilia Romagna, Tuscany, Umbria, Le Marche, Lazio and Abruzzo.

All of this exemplifies how difficult it is to write a book about buying a property in Italy. Even the laws are different in various places. I can't tell you where you will be happy, but can make the process of buying a happier one, and if knowledge is bliss, maybe even a smugly contented one.

So Italy it is – what do you want to buy?

It's rare that a househunter doesn't have an idea about what they want. Much more usual is the client who has spent the last 12 interminable Northern winters nurturing the Italian dream, and when they arrive they know exactly what they want, down to the address, the colour of the cushions and the fact they won't compromise on anything.

Follow the lessons learnt from reality television over the last 20 years, location, location location. Make a list. What is most important to you? What's most important to your other half? The kids? The dog? Argue, make another list – and by the time the snow melts you will have a short list of must haves, and a longer list of 'quite likes'. Putting aside essentials such as proximity to a Yehudi Menuhin school, or being within 3 minutes of an international airport you can concentrate on the substance of your search.   So what's most important?: sea, sea view, countryside, town…

Sea: Italy has 7600km of coastline – the vast part unpopulated and unspoilt – but you can't have a house on the beach – at least, if it doesn't already legally exist. The law does not allow any new building within 150 metres of the sea so if you want a front line property in a country meets sea zone – you're going to have to buy at least a couple of hectares of land and build at the back of the lot.   Don't believe anyone who tells you differently. (Some regions, such as Sardinia have a 300 metre zone, others 200 metres – the national minimum is 150metres, unless you are friendly with the mayor of your village and bung him a few euros. All 'legal' villas that have sprung up in the south of Italy seem to belong to leading local politicians – a perfect example of the law being more equal for some than others.)

History: In the south the only people who built on the sea were poor fishermen – so its not easy to find older larger properties at the sea. Amalfi perhaps is the honorable exception having been a maritime power in the late middle ages. Other ports have older quarters such as Bari, Taranto and Catania, but noble houses were nearly always built in the hills. North of Rome there are many ports and towns on the sea and you will be in competition with Italian second home buyers from the suburbs of Rome and Milan for your weekend hideaway.

Buyers fall into two groups. Those who want a sea view and those who don't. You can have sea views from 20km inland if you're lucky, but half the people want a house within 3 or 4km of the sea, with a 180 degree view, and these inevitably carry a premium, especially as you're in direct competition with Italians.

If you're happy living more than 300m from the sea prices drop – most Italians at 500m would feel the need to drive to the beach – if you're buying in a resort seriously think about getting a property with a garage or private parking because in the summer you'll have to get up at 5am to get a parking space.

Out of towns and up to 7/8km from the sea, prices drop further, but a sea view is still a must for alot of people – even better if its panoramic and consists only of sea – the more holiday homes, supermarkets and cement factories that block your view the more the price is negotiable. Also bear in mind that Italians like living cheek by jowel with neighbours – its friendly. Slowly they are beginning to understand that foreigners like their privacy – but its all comparative – a house may be sold with a private terrace, that in reality is separated from the neighbours' by a dead pot plant. There is complete incomprehension that someone would want to buy a house with no other property in view - and slowly after years in Italy I'm inclined to agree. Neighbours are good – especially nosy ones who live there all year round – believe me! You will never go short of fresh fruit, any visitors who come in your absence will be fingerprinted and checked, and your personal life will be the subject of endless discussion by your neighbours and anyone who happens to be passing.

Neighbours are more important if you're thinking of buying in the country – remember that water, electricity and other services are optional in many parts of the countryside – and someone to keep an eye on your property when you're not there is worth their weight in gold – or at least olives. Italians don't generally buy in the country, so country homes are comparatively much cheaper than by the sea, and the house comes second to the land included in the sale. At the risk of sounding derogatory – it's a peasant society – and useful land is worth much more than a falling down barn that a prospective buyer thinks could be a super loft style conversion. On that basis level good soil is worth a lot more than terraced rock – even if it's less picturesque. Land and houses near to towns, on an asphalted road, obviously carry a premium. If a house seems unreasonably cheap, there's a reason. A house with 13 hectares in a beautiful valley with sea views may seem a bargain at 100.000 euros, but you have to ford a river to get there and there is absolutely no building allowed at all. 100 grand for a property you can't reach in the winter and you can't restore isn't such good value. Obviously in regions such Tuscany where new build is a complete no-no a registered building has an intrinsic value, and here price guides fail woefully. A old farmhouse on the Senese Crete will have a price tag that takes into account that the view will never change, and for a new build apartment you'll have to schlep over to Poggibonsi.

Holiday Homes or Relocation?

There are those who want a holiday home for up to six months a year, and those that want to come here for good. The blurry bit is the client who wants a holiday home and within a few years will cut all ties with home and settle here to see out their earthly days.

The requirements are not usually wildly different. However, for those who spend their prêt a manger lunch hours dreaming of strimmers, rotovators and harvesting 13 types of tomato, the next section is for you:

Self sufficiency.

Buy a good strimmer – at least 4Hp – anything else will slice off a bit of grass, but as soon as it sees a thistle it will splutter and feign illness.

Buy a good rotovator – diesel and 10 Hp – it may pull your arms out of their sockets, but it will do the job that some wimpy little petrol thing can never manage.

Chainsaw, pick, hoe, and rake, and if you can run to it a small tractor. If you have more than 1 hectare a tractor is devoutly to be wished for.

It may seem picturesque, but terraced land is not easy to farm, inasmuch as access is never easy, and you could spend more time cultivating a talent for rebuilding dry stone walls than sleeping. The self sufficient year will pan out like this:

Almond harvest – late August/early September

Carob harvest – September / October

Citrus Harvest – October to March/June varieties depending

Vendemmia (grape harvest) - Mid september

Olive Harvest – October/November

Pruning trees and cleaning land, chopping firewood – September – December

Repairing roads/dry stone walls after heavy rains: Jan – March, Sept – December

Cleaning land to prevent fire hazards April/May

Preparing vines, fertilising, pruning – March/April.

Watering : June – September

Planting, weeding, growing and reaping – September to July.

So you can see that the first two weeks of August you can have a rest, unless you have livestock.

If you are planning on being truly self sufficient it's a good idea to buy your land and set yourself up as 'agricoltore' – which doesn't mean you're a fully fledged farmer, but does bring you some incentives. If you want to go the whole hog and open an azienda agricola – (a proper farm) you can get even more incentives, but the paperwork rises proportionally. The most usual incentives are for planting olive and/or carob trees, and raising rare breeds of cow, pig, sheep or the Ragusano donkey – which is reason enough, frankly, to go through the paperwork.

If you fancy the idea of keeping a couple of sheep and a pig, you just need to check what your region allows. Some will allow 3 goats and 1 pig, others only two. As long as they are small beasts and fit into the peasant farming scheme of things, you will be allowed something. A cow on the other hand requires alot of paperwork and a licence.

If on the other hand, your thoughts run to opening an agriturismo, you will need an advisor to help you get the available funds. If you don't want to sell what you grow, you can plump for rural tourism as a business, which comes with different rules, different funds and different signposts. Whatever you decide to do, competition is fierce, so you need to do something that makes you stand out from the crowd. Stuff like painting holidays, photography holidays, learning how to dry stone wall, cook, make a scale model of a Greek temple or hold up a bank type holidays are very popular at the moment, and if you can corner the market in 'activity' holidays (which to me seem a contradiction in terms), you could be onto a winner.

As I said earlier, people who come on holiday to Italy don't want to slum it, so do as Richard and Sarah did in Tuscany, and realise early on that you can't let out a clean shed at the bottom of the garden. The greener you can be, the better. Think photo voltaics, water saving, recycling (riciclaggio), organic food (cibo biologico), and so on. It will take a greater initial outlay, but the rewards in both visitors and tax breaks will be worth it.

The most frequently asked questions...

Will I have a problem with the mafia/camorra/'ndrangheta or organized crime in general?

If you're planning on importing large amounts of drugs from abroad, running a prostitution ring or setting up slot machine arcades, mixing a lot of cement, or opening a branch of Ikea, then yes, it's likely you might get a knock on your door. If however, your ideas turn more towards buying a house and living in it, its highly doubtful you're going to be important enough for organized crime to take an interest. Most peoples' idea of the mafia is still that of Marlon Brando falling over amongst his tomatoes at the end of the Godfather. It's not like that. What it is will almost certainly never be anything to do with you, at least not directly. Italy has more organized crime that any other western country, and it will touch your life at some point whether you live in Venice, Rome or Taormina. You certainly won't find a man in a pin stripe suit casually brandishing a violin case on the street corner, but you will undoubtedly meet the 'omertà' – the 'I know nothing' mentality. Strangely it's not true – Italians know everything – mainly because they are compulsive gossips - they just choose not to tell you. You are much more likely to see the small scale crime: pickpockets, fake dvds, 'real' Gucci bags for a fiver, etc that is still run by the larger organizations especially in the big cities.

What's the water situation?

The south of Italy is dry – in Sicily it usually doesn't rain between June and September. At all. However, there is water, and goodly amounts of it. It all depends who is in charge of distributing it. If you're living in the country, get a cistern – at least for rainwater. This has a double advantage – the winter rains fill up the cistern and you're set for most of the summer, and you can always top it up by getting a bowser to come out. Also the new laws on energy efficiency will give you a higher grading for recycling and saving water. You can always ask permission to sink a borehole – it depends where you are, though as a rule of thumb you can't sink a well if there's another one within 150 metres. Boreholes for agricultural use are now difficult to sink. More usual is domestic use, which will give you a licence for about 0.5 litres a second, which is more than adequate unless you are planning an Alton Towers water park in your back garden. In the north, water isnt generally a problem, the towns have good mains water and the comunes are much more adept at running the infrastructure. Once you get up in the mountains you may have to rely on a rainwater cistern and a bowser, but the locals manage it so there's no reason why a tourist can't.

2021 was a strange year climatewise. Whether this is El Nino or a long term change in weather patterns depends on which newspaper you read. What is pretty evident over the last ten years or so is that extreme weather is more common. Gone are the days of a constant drizzle, now it's all or nothing. Alot of this is dependent on sea temperatures, and the Med is certainly heating up - you only have to see the type of fish which are spotted to know that the tropics are not as far away as they used to be. And with warmer seas come strange weather patterns. The impact of this on Italy will be huge in the longer term. In the more immediate future, the homebuyer needs to be sure that the house they are contemplating isnt in a zone subject to landslip (frana), that the geologists report on water flow shows that the house is not slap bang in the middle of a watercourse when it rains alot, and that you're preferably a good few metres above sea level. Ideally you will have your own limitless water supply and not plant thirsty crops such as kiwi fruit.

As I write in late January, the River Po is at a lower level than in summer. It's not just the south which is going to have severe water problems in the future. If you are planning on buying a renovating a property anywhere in Italy you should allocate time and money on a system of water saving and re-use.

How about earthquakes/volcanoes /landslides?

Well, yes – they happen. You have to develop a bit of the Mediterranean fatality – if it happens at least you've eaten well. However, earthquakes are unpredictable – there are well over 500 a year in Italy, of varying dimensions, from Venice down to Sicily, and nobody can tell you where and how big the next one will be. Volcanoes are fortunately more visible, and easier not to buy a house on one. Landslides are currently the biggest killer in Italy – years of underfunding and ignoring the problems have meant that last year heavy rains in Liguria, Sicily, Campania, and Calabria have washed away entire towns and killed too many people. The reasons are many – without doubt, illegal building is one of them, as is deforestation. Buying a house on a vertical hillside may look pretty but it's asking for trouble. You can get hold of the regional maps of hydro-geological risk which will show every single place where there is a danger of landslip but, unfortunately, that is no guarantee of anything. Again in the last few years there have been devastating heavy rains in Ligura, Emilia, Veneto and Piemonte. The warming of the

Mediterranean and the cold fronts coming in from the Atlantic mean that this is not a temporary problem, and will only get worse. Genova has been particularly badly hit, and exemplifies terrible urban planning, building on flood plains and a lack of maintenance of the rivers and sewers. Again the rule here is look around and don't leave your brain behind when you make a decision.

Is it safe?

Going out and leaving the door wide open isn't advised anywhere nowadays, and the same is true of Italy. Being sensible and having a well secured property is common sense. Most crime is opportunistic, but a house that is locked up for most of the year may well invite unwelcome scrutiny, especially if it is very isolated. Some people make great play of having the 'ronde' check the property, but its not always the best solution. A good alarm system which phones someone in the area and which makes A LOT of noise is the best bet.

Obviously in the larger cities it's not the best idea to leave keys in your door, and pickpockets are a menace. When visiting these cities, keep your money in a zipped inside pocket and don't flaunt expensive watches and jewellery.

Undoubtedly Italy is not as safe as it once was - small towns in the country offer the best security, as do small islands.

Basically, places where everyone knows everyone else offer an unofficial neighbourhood watch.

Is the driving as bad as they say?

It's worse, but it's still better than Naples. Southern Italians drive with joy – each driver is Lewis Hamilton and on a private circuit that miraculously takes him to his destination. If you are going to be overtaken on a suicidal bend it will be an Audi that screams past. Any two lane road is implicitly regarded as being 4 lane, and you will learn that soon enough. Drive on the right. Right on the right. Roundabouts are the living equivalent of some hideous shoot'em up video game. Solid white lines in the middle of the road mean nothing. Italian drivers may appear aggressive, but they're not in the road rage league. The most that will happen will be a lot of gesticulation and eyes cast to heaven. If a car is within inches of your rear bumper and flashing his lights it's only because he wants to get home for lunch and can't understand why you don't want to overtake on a blind bend with a huge lorry driving right at you.

Avoid driving in big southern cities if at all possible. Don't tailgate. Indicators are optional extras and usually activated only after the manouvre has started.

In the north driving is much more regulated. On the other hand there are speed cameras every half mile, and you can quite easily get enough points on your licence to incur a ban merely by driving to work.   When the Northerners come on holiday to the soũth they adopt southern driving within seconds - it's genetic, indicators, parking bays and speed limits become annoying distractions to using your phone while driving.

All over Italy signposting is dire. Roads are designated on their termination point, so a road in Bologna may have a sign saying Naples, but nothing in between.

A seriously good thing to remember is that if you park in a service station, large car park, or big city don't lock your car with the remote beep beep thing. Use the key. There are stories, and personal experiences, where as you lock your car the radio frequency is copied by a naughty man in the area, and you return to your car to find it locked and secure, but lacking important things like money, passports and desirable dogs/children/suitcases.

Do I need a lawyer?

Not if you use a good estate agent — There are plenty of international lawyers firms around who promise you the earth for a not inconsiderable consideration.   The work that a lawyer sitting in London will do is translate the documents, ask some questions, and run off some visure from the computer in his office. He will do nothing that a good estate agent and a decent notaio (notary) won't do. Obviously, if you are planning on buying a property that is mortgaged to the hilt via an offshore company I'd say use a lawyer, but for a straightforward sale it really isn't necessary.

A word about the law. You may know Bleak House and the story of the infinite corridors of Chancery, and how Jarndyce and his companions became lost in the maze of law that Dickens drew so devastatingly. Take Bleak House – it's a ladybird book in comparison to Italian civil law. Not only does the Italian system grind so slowly as to be invisible to the naked eye, it is chronically underfunded, lacks personnel, a system and any sense of logic. I have had 3 brushes with

Italian law – initial brushes because unlike in the Uk where the small claims court would have sorted it out in 10 minutes flat, here we are locked to a process that after 2 years has completed only the first hearing. And nothing happens at the first hearing, other than the judge puts everything on hold for a couple of months, because – well because nothing gets decided at the first hearing. Then there's the choice of court, choice of judge and choice of words – it's not enough to go to the local tribunale – I was cited by a non agent for unfair competition – (unfair to what? He's a tobacconist and I don't sell cigarettes) – he summonsed me to the local tribunal, my lawyer had the 'trial' redirected because his lawyer had named a judge who wasn't qualified to listen to the complex arguments, and now it's going to Catania because they know more about commercial law than the bumpkins in Modica. A year on, and precisely nothing has happened, other than the lawyer has lot of my money. Avoid Italian law if you can, it will drive you pottier than Miss Flite and her caged birds….

Are there bargains to be found?

No. There are well priced properties, but bargains disappeared a while ago. If there is some bargain to be had, you will not get it – usually an estate agent or relative/friend of the seller will buy it and then sell it on at market price. Think about it – why should you, who has no local knowledge and no contacts get a property at a bargain price before relatives, friends and local businessmen who know exactly what is on the market and for how much? Since the last crisis however, there are those who really need to sell, and they will accept brazen offers. It's a fine line between a negotiation and an insult and in the latter case the seller could well refuse to have anything more to do with you.

Estate Agents

There are 3 sorts of estate agent in Italy.

> Legal and good.

> Legal and bad

> Illegal.

Let's start with the legal ones. In all of Italy, you can't be an estate agent unless you've passed exams and got your licence. This is designed to protect the public and in some areas it works. The theory is sound. An estate agent is independent and works for both parties to finalise the transaction. As such he will take commission from both parties. Italians love the 'trattativa' – the arguing over nuances and the endless argy bargy over price.

You can only be really sure that your agent is legal if he or she is a member of FIAIP, (Federazione Italiana Agenti Immobiliare

Professionali), the professional body. The agent must be nominated and seconded by other FIAIP members to get in, and once in you pay a fortune for the privilege. Fiaip agents have a code of conduct, and more importantly, insurance in case they make a mess of it all and leave a client baying for blood.

The other large professional association – FIMAA – is also technically only for legal, licenced estate agents, but they also give membership to the bloke who owns the tobacconist and sells houses on the side – so unfortunately FIMAA no longer has the kudos it once had.

ANAMA is the Associazione Nazionale Agenti e Mediatori d'Affari and like FIMAA is an arm of a National business council – the Conferescenti, or in FIMAA's case the Confcommercio – and both represent not only estate agents, but also financial agents and mediators of all types.

As far as real estate agencies themselves go, the big franchises are growing in power and presence. Tecnocasa was the biggest in Italy, but I have to say that the branches I have visited have been pretty poor. The latest all consuming franchise is ReMax, which operates on a strange system of one agent and dozens of 'consulente' who are only paid commission on sales. Just buying the name isn't enough to guarantee a good level of service, and the franchising system in Italy means that it's a cunning way round the law, as you can have a franchise without necessarily being a licenced agent. Even the odd foreign franchise has landed, such as Engels and Wolkers who promise much, charge 4% commission and have yet to make real inroads into the market but insist on exclusive contracts to the detriment of all and sundry. It all comes down to the individual agency that you use.

Even some legal estate agents are not the upstanding citizens they should be. It is illegal for an estate agent to profit from the deal other than from his commission, but this doesn't stop some selling their own property, signing compromessos and flipping a property, or taking back handers from the seller to get a higher price from the buyers. It is rife. If you're asked to sign a compromesso with a different person from the owner of the property, there is usually something going on.

Unfortunately it's not easy to know whether your estate agent is good at his job until it's too late, but by the time you've seen a few properties you should have a clear idea if he knows what he is talking about.

Illegal agents fall into two camps: the ones who pretend to be legal agents and have offices and web sites, and the bloke you meet on a street corner who happens to know someone who has a house to sell. Neither of these has the right to ask for commission, and it is illegal to give it to them without it being declared in the act of sale.

There are some particularly glossy websites about offering houses and legal advice. All omit the words 'agenzia immobiliare' and usually promise a team of professionals who offer legal assistance. Basically this means that the agency is a lawyers office, out to make a bit more money. It doesn't make sense buying a house from the same lawyer who will prepare your contract – it's just asking for trouble. It's also illegal for a lawyer to act as an estate agent. They can lose their licence to practice the law – there is obviously a vast conflict of interests at work. Any lawyer who sells houses should be reported – he won't ask for commission – they get around this particular problem by including their commission in their legal fees – but it's a slippery slope to take, and again, you end up with no protection if things go awry.

Some 'agents' have the back up of another legal estate agent – technically it's not allowed – even the man who shows you the house should be a registered estate agent. The Civil code states that an agent must be independent, impartial and not tied by obligation, collaboration or representation to either the buyer or the seller. If the agent himself or his partner is making money by selling you a property (other than their legitimate commission) they can lose their licence and pay hefty fines – so don't be afraid to trot off the to the carabinieri or the Guardia di Finanza if you smell a rat. Just because it's Italy doesn't mean you will 'end up with the fishes' – the vast majority of Italians abhor dishonesty and lament how these agents give the region a bad name.

Basically the rule of thumb is that if your agent doesn't want to be named in the act of sale he's acting illegally – it means that you, he and possibly the notaio are breaking the law and can all be fined. Worst of all as the buyer you have absolutely no comeback if things aren't what they seem.

Obviously, if the first you know about it is at the point of act, something has gone awry, so on first meeting an agent ask to see his or her credentials – a legal agent will have no problem! Many ex-provinces are now issuing photocards to legal agents as a form of ID. Other than that ask to see their membership card for FIAIP or FIMAA, and if that isn't forthcoming ask to see proof of their inscription at the Chamber of Commerce. From May 2012 the role of estate agent disappeared, but they must be registered in the REA (the register of businesses) and the Chamber of Commerce should issue shiny plastic cards to all legal estate agents which will act as a type of licence. The REA number is written into the act of sale by the notaio and should also be on the front page of the agents website.

Any agent must put his licence number on the front page of his website along with his VAT /IVA number. Again this isn't as easy as it should be. A tobacconist will have a licence number with the local Chamber of Commerce – the Camera di Commercio – but it doesn't mean that he can also sell houses. If he's a member of FIAIP he's legal, but make sure his dues are paid for the current year.

With the general economic malaise, many legit agents have suspended their VAT number but continue to run their office and work under the radar. It means that they will want to be paid in cash, and again this is not in your interest.

NEW LAWS ON ABUSIVI

There is now a law on illegal agents which increases the fines for all parties who use an illegal agent and pay in cash. Not only - it will also impose jail sentences (thereby becoming a criminal act and not a civil crime), and can involve the sequestration of goods (ie the house bought through the illegal agent). Needless to add - do not use illegal agents, do not pay in 'nero' and make sure that your agent is cited fully with the amount paid to him in the act of purchase when it is stipulated at the notaio. Paying an agent in 'nero' is only costing you money and legal protection. To re-emphasise the point: Your agent, whoever it is, MUST be cited in the act of the sale with the amount of commission paid. If not you are breaking the law, you could get a 15.000 euro fine and have your act annulled. When the new law is rubber stamped, you could also lose your house!.

FOREIGN AGENTS

You'll see a large number of British, American, and assorted sites that are based in a different country and offer property for sale in Italy. Sorting out the wheat from the chaff is a virtually impossible task.

A British company which has a website with property in Italy is unlikely to be an Italian estate agent. These listing sites which offer the Dolce Vita will want paying in the country where they are based, and will not want to appear in the act of sale. The agent in Italy will act, and be paid for, solely by the seller - and therefore you have absolutely no legal recourse in the event of mistakes.   In such cases you should pay your commission to the agent on the ground in Italy which will be written into the act of sale, and the English listing agent can then invoice him for his share after the event.

 The English sites have their place, but remember that the majority are listings for agents or for a bloke who flogs houses. They earn the buyers commission for sending an email, and you will probably pay more than the local level of commission – so its not the most cost effective way to shop for a house, and an Italian estate agent will always prefer a direct contact to a referral.

There's an American lawyer who has a large internet presence and who says he is allowed to sell property in Italy as he is lawyer.   He isn't, and what's worse he obviously knows nothing about the law.   If you pay his astronomical consultancy fees you will end up unhappy and poorer.

Agents who are based in Italy, but use any number of other terms to describe themselves such as a portal for buyers, a buyers' agent, consultants, property specialists, or a holiday rental company who sell houses on the side are very unlikely to be legal, and it is entirely at your risk if you give them lots of money and get nothing in return. What is important to remember is that only a legal agent has the right to ask for and get commission. You are under no legal obligation to give anyone else a cent. Some offices will market themselves as consultants – consulente – and this is just another way to get round the law. A consulente will act for both parties and call his commission a fee – it doesn't mean you are protected in any way – and the likelihood is the consultant knows nothing about what he's talking about other than the price of the property.

The law requires that any agent involved in the sale of a property is named in the final act of sale. This is mainly for the law on recycling of money – and you should say how much the agent has been paid, along with his number of inscription and partita IVA/VAT number – all so the Guardia di Finanza can keep tabs on them. If you don't name and shame the agent – usually because he doesn't want to be put in the act it has potential consequences.   Firstly you will have technically committed perjury, ie – made a false declaration in a public act – and that carries a fine for you of up to 10.000 euros, and since last year a possible prison sentence. Secondly, you sign away any right of recourse in the unhappy event that something is wrong. If there is no agent in the act, the law says there was never an agent involved in the sale, so you have no-one to sue. Not naming the agent saves him a lot of money - his entire commission becomes tax free, but it only saves you the VAT on his fee. It is not a gamble worth taking.

Commission:

The rate of commission in Italy is technically 'advised' by the Chamber of Commerce in the province where the estate agent has his legal seat. It's now a rate of 3% or 4% and is technically set by the 'use and custom' of the area - so if a goodly amount of agents ask 3% then 3% it is. One agent near me asks for 6% from the buyer on the basis that he will obtain your codice fiscale – it must be the best paid 10 mins work of the year for him. Minimum and maximum tariffs are being abolished, so it's worth asking your agent how much the commission will be before you start. Better still, the rate should be clearly written on the website. The big cities such as Rome and Milan have a different set of rules. If it's a buyers' market you can negotiate with the agent about how much commission he will charge. Make sure whatever is agreed is in writing, as the default position is always in the agents' favour. Also agree the rate of commission before you make the offer on the property, once done you have no more bargaining power. Even in tiny towns in Molise it seems that the agents have called each other and agreed on unified fees – in one case a minimum of 3000 euros (plus IVA) for a purchase – which means paying 3600 odd euros for a house which may cost less than 10.000 euros.

The easiest way to find an estate agent is using one of the big sites such as www.immobiliare.it or www.idealista.it – checking out the individual agents web site and then doing a further check – a FIAIP agent will be listed on the FIAIP site – www.fiaip.it or alternatively go to the Chamber of Commerce site – www.registroimprese.it and check if the agent is registered with the REA – you can search by category – either agente immobiliare or agenzia immobiliare or directly by name. An agente immobiliare is a sole trader so you might have to look him up by name, whereas an agenzia is a company and will be found by the company name. If they're not on this site, they are not legal - though the site itself is only in Italian and notoriously difficult to navigate.

There's another new site: the catchily named https://www.agentiimmobiliariabilitati.it/ and putting the region and city will bring up all the legal agents in that area.

Being on a site such as casa.it or immobiliare.it should technically be open only to legally operating agents, but it's never so simple. Always check the credentials of the agency before you shortlist them – it's the quickest and simplest way to save yourselves a lot of money and heartache.

If you end up buying using an illegal agent – the most important thing to remember is to refuse point blank to pay his fee at any point before the act of sale. The Italian civil code and custom in various parts have the commission payable at compromesso (the preliminary of sale) – because according to the Civil Code – 'the affair has been concluded at this point' In the olden days of yore perhaps it was the case that the handshake and deposit concluded the affair, nowadays its not quite so black and white. Pay commission at the final act, or afterwards – the illegal agent hasn't got a leg to stand on as 1) they are not entitled to any commission 2) the payment will be in 'nero' and undoubtedly cash only and 3) you're paying.

Also, don't do anything else illegal such underdeclaring – should the Guardia di Finanza descend on the illegal agent, you as a client will also be hounded down and have to pay fines for making false declarations in a public act – at 10.000 euros a time they can soon add up.

A ruling of the High Court has recently said that if a third party asks for his money back from an illegal agent, it has to be paid over without a word of protest. Quite how this is done without a massive police presence and dogs is beyond me.

Commission paid (legally) to an estate agent is tax deductible if you submit an IRPEF (income tax) return. You can claim up to 1000 euros on the commission incurred on buying a prima casa.

I've got two days to find my dream home....

That's what it boils down to. It doesn't matter how many months you've spent scrolling through agents sites, when you're on the ground you've got a limited amount of time to find the house you've thought about for the last goodness knows how long. Estate agents take your money, so make them earn it. Be as specific as possible about what you want – I've lost count of the amount of times people land in my office without knowing anything either about Italy or about the house they want to buy. At the risk of sounding fuddy duddy and old fashioned – buy a book. Oh you have done – buy another one then.

So, the upshot of all of this is - know where you want to buy. It sounds simple but it isn't. The heart will ultimately rule the head – and you need to drive around and see where you feel comfortable, and if that somewhere can give you the shops, the restaurants, the schools, the medical facilities that you need, then you've hit the jackpot. Usually there will be a compromise.

I plumped for the south east of Sicily because it was so friendly. The people are completely different from the

Palermitani or the Trapanesi. And its green – very green. Its as if the south east corner collects all Sicilian water – and in April its like an English high summer but with wild flower meadows, butterflies and eagles. Rural England but with sun and no pesticides – like a film with Joan Plowright. - I knew Siracusa and was bowled over by its beauty, but knew I didn't want to live there, so used it as a base to explore a bit. When I came to Modica I knew within 30 seconds I had come home.

Once you've at least zoned in to a province, you can start to make your estate agent work for his money. But be specific – the more you help him, the less of your time he's going to waste. As most people buy in Italy after doing a bit of research, you can get a good idea of what's available and prices by searching the internet. Don't just use the English sites – the biggest of the Italian sites are user friendly and you don't need a degree in Italian to navigate them. Nowadays most of the 'annunci' are in English too.

The biggest site in Sicily (and Italy) is now www.idealista.it which has bought up casa.it, followed by www.immobiliare.it Smaller but guaranteed in that all the agents listed are FIAIP members is www.cercacasa.it . Some foreign sites are worth visiting, though many agents can't afford the extortionate fees of realmovingproperty or somesuch. Personally I use gate-away.com. Of course, contacting a Italian estate agent directly is no guarantee that you'll get a response. Emails are treated by many agents in the same way that you would treat a cold caller trying to sell you a conservatory if you live in a fourth floor flat. However, a serious estate agent will respond – eventually.

So you've found a house on the net and you've sent an email asking for details. Italians will love you if you try to speak Italian, adore you if you write it – so try something along the lines of

Gentile Signore,

Ho visto suo annuncio sul www.casa.it Rif: Villa al mare. Può inviarmi più dettagli e il prezzo, se è ancora in vendita.

Cordiali saluti

A. Househunter.

Alternatively make a check list of Italian words that are indispensable in your search – closeness to a school, mains water, distance from the sea, private parking and so on and add them into your email in a second catch all sentence:

Può anche farmi sapere la scuola (elementare/media/superiore) più vicina, se c'è acqua comunale, distanza dal mare, se c'è parcheggio privato ...

You'll see that se c'è means "if there's" and its a useful catch all for non countable nouns!

If this all fails you and you really don't want to practice your Italian on an Italian, write in English – most younger Italians can read ok, it's the talking that does them in..at least in the south where mother-tongue English teachers are a rare and precious commodity.

English sites that cater for an exclusive English speaking market will almost undoubtedly be more expensive than bilingual or Italian sites – watch that the prices are displayed in both languages on a bilingual site – its not unusual for the English prices to be displayed and theres nothing in Italian – local agents adding a premium for the foreign customer. There is also no guarantee that they know their job.

When I first arrived in Sicily I tried the following: walk into local estate agent and ask for properties for less than 40.000 euros – the reply – 'You wont even find a cave for less than 40.000 euros' As in the best cartoons I could see the dollar signs in the slot machine eyes of the woman behind the desk who refused to even show me a house until I had signed an exclusive agreement with the agency.

Enter my Sicilian mate with the same question – the computer turned on and a list of possible properties displayed in full slideshow mode. It was one of the fundamental reasons I became an estate agent – to stuff the hideous woman and her over evident greed.

I have never trusted an estate agent anywhere who doesn't show the prices of the houses on their site.

Until a few years ago, Italian estate agents worked on the principle that they knew best. You'd ask about a house, and then jump in his car and go and see the houses he wanted to sell you – he knew what you wanted, and you had no say in the matter. It would cut no mustard with a northern European, so times they have a-changed.

They still know best, but let you think they don't.

In fact you won't find an Italian who doesn't know what you want, what you think and what you ought to think. You will never meet a southern Italian who apologises – he may come close, but you won't get the all important 'sorry'. In fact most English who speak Italian are perennially admonished because we say 'scusi' too much. Most of all you will never meet a Italian who doesn't know where to eat and how to cook – even if they've never picked up a spatula in their lives – its part of the genes – all conversations wind up with being about food.

I remember following two hulking great football supporters down the street, and they were discussing the game – 'But that pass- he should have stayed on the bench'

'It was a rubbish game'

'Yeah'

'Did you have those snacks at half time?'

'Yes , they were exquisite, but they were a bit over salted'

'Yeah, they should have lightly toasted them before serving – it would have brought out the flavours'

The protestant work ethic of north Europe and the new world hits the buffers in south Italy. A telephone call, which in London could be dispatched in 2 minutes, here takes fifteen. I am suffered rather than celebrated because I refuse to bloat Telecom's already huge profits by chatting about nothing on the phone. After the necessary introductions, I want to talk business – it is after all the reason for the call, but it's hard going. More often than not, my determined blinkered approach will dissolve in the face of a lengthy monologue about the fish that was eaten the other day or a morbid willingness to tell me about medical problems of people whose name I don't even know. Italy has a love affair with mobile phones and all their hideous accessories. Pensioners are adept at sending SMS, a phone that rings takes preference over anyone standing at a counter, and a virulent desire for twee ringtones has overtaken the population. I am happy to stick to my Anglo Saxon guns and use the phone when necessary and for short a time as possible, in the vague and fruitless hope that others may appreciate my brevity. I know it's futile. Italians love to talk.

Let's assume you've found an estate agent who replies to your emails, and you've let them know what you are looking for – a two bed town house, with a view, a terrace and letting potential, to modernize.

Reading between the lines in Italian is the same as in English, but the lines are further apart. Two bedrooms can mean anything from a long corridor with a curtain down the middle, to an understairs cupboard with a cot and a shoebox. This is why Italians attach great importance to the overall square metrage of the property. You may say two bedrooms, but to an Italian knowing the house is 55 square metres, means he can work out how much sleeping space there is – just don't ask me how. Italian estate agents will rhapsodise over a view of a sewage works – it is after all not a brick wall a metre from your window. I'm beginning to suspect they just see things differently to other people. If your uncontaminated sea view is a cement factory with the sea just visible through the fire escape – your estate agent will tell you how nice it is to have neighbours who work regular hours, and should you want a a bag of gesso, you only have to hoik it over the wall – what more could you ask for? A terrace is infinitely variable – from a window sill to something the size of a football pitch: letting potential ? Of course. And then we come to the dreaded word modernize. I choose the 'm' word if the house has a kitchen and bathroom, but time has stood still since 1973 – and the mocha bathroom suite is in situ. Other agents might say 3 stones and a dried up well befit the term modernize, but be warned – it's a subjective thing, and trust the photos rather than the agent on this one.

Ah, yes – photos. With the demise of the sole agency contract a lot of agents have decided not to put accurate photos on the website, convinced that the competition will either steal them or go and find the house and persuade the owner to let them sell it instead. It is possible that the house you fall in love with on the net was in fact sold some years ago or is in a different town. Ask the agent if the photos on the website are of the property you are planning to visit. You won't always find internal photos on the web either – probably the owners don't want all and sundry looking at their ornaments, but if you ask the agent should send you them.

What's your budget?

Most people don't trust an estate agent who asks them what their budget is. They fear that if they say, 'up to 250.000 euros' every property shown to them will be miraculously, 249.000 euros. If the agent has prices on his website, you know he's telling porkies at this point. From the agent's point of view it's the most pertinent question – if he knows your budget he knows what you can afford and wont waste your and his time with houses that only raise or lower your expectations.

An agent WILL ask you at some point how much you want to spend – if not he will assume your budget from what you ask to see. As in the UK or anywhere, a two bedroom house can veer from 30.000 for a pile of rubble to 2 million if it's in the most desirable spot on the planet and was owned by Julia Roberts – so you really have to swallow hard and tell the agent how much you want to spend. Deep breath, go on – say the words.

It's easy in these heady days of hyper text transfer protocol to know a vague market price for a property. 10 minutes on a website will give you an idea of how much a modern 2 bed flat in a town centre should cost you. Similarly its easy for the agent to know that if you say you're a Italian property expert but can only talk about a long weekend you had in Venice, he may suspect that you're gilding your lily a bit. What Im trying to say is be honest with your agent. Its true he wants you to buy, otherwise he goes hungry, but he also wants you to be happy, recommend him to your friends and not write vile things about him on your blog – So help him and he'll help you – and some agents will do much more than their duty to land you your dream home.

Immobiliare.it and some other portals now offer valuations (stime). All you have to do is put in the address and the site will tell you how much a house is worth. Obviously its a pathetic marketing ploy. There is no differentiation between restored or uninhabitable, location, or pertinences.

Buy to Let - Holiday Homes

It seems easy – buy a house, bung it on the internet and make a packet from people less fortunate than you. If only it were so.

If you're thinking of buying to let you need to know how much you need in yearly rental to break even. Then halve it. That's your budget. If you're buying a property for yourself and the idea of renting it out to cover the running costs appeals, that's one thing, making it a business with an income is another pair of sleeves entirely, as they say in Italy.

My opinion, for what you may think it's worth is:

If you're buying a family house in the country, you will not let it if it doesn't have a pool. It's that simple.

Swimming pools are not cheap to run, but they do let you double a rent – bear in mind that you will be paying for maintenance even when the house is not let. The market is generally for couples and small families, or large groups. A three bedroom house is perfect for a smaller investment, something that sleeps 12-16 for a larger.

Property management companies are many and various. The bigger companies will guarantee let periods, but it means that you probably can't go when you would like to, and they take more than half of your rent. The smaller companies will charge less, but cannot guarantee a fully booked period, so some of the work remains with you. If you want a totally hands off approach use one of the bigger companies.

Competition is fierce, especially round the bigger tourist resorts such as Siena, Taormina and Lecce. Town centres have loads of case vacanze, bed and breakfast, and affittacamere, the trick is here is to set yourself apart from the crowd and do something chic and modern – you probably wont get much more in rent, but you will rent for longer periods.

The letting period in south Italy is from Easter to October, with some places having a high season at Christmas. High season is June/July and September. 'Altissima' season is August, unless you're nowhere near the sea or a famous city. North of Rome it starts later, finishes earlier, but with a ski slope nearby you can add a couple of months in the winter. Places like Florence may have a dip in February, but that's about it. The lesson learnt from the last couple of years is budget for the minimum number of weeks you need. If you lash out on a property that necessitates letting for 30 weeks a year, you could end up very badly burned.

Don't dismiss the 'owners' direct' websites – such a Holiday lettings, Homelidays, Villa renters, owners direct and so on – your letting agent can't really advertise on these, and they cost 300 euros per year, or thereabouts, and it doesn't mean that you have to deal with the enquiries – just forward them to your letting agent.

The trick with all rents is to make the property appealing – a lot of people think that a kitchen filled with white plastic garden furniture is fine. It isn't. Think about what you would like to find in a fairly expensive holiday rental and apply those rules. Your management agent will undoubtedly have a list of things you need to put in the house.

Sofa–beds don't count as beds for northern European tourists. A 4'6" bed or sofa bed in Italy is a large single, don't try letting it as a double, people will ask for their money back.

Included by necessity nowadays is internet access. If you don't want to install a fixed line, make an internet key/mofi available to guests – it's a low outlay that brings a high reward. Many clients now specify that internet must be present in the house, and internet points aren't widely available in large parts of the peninsular. There are zillions of ways to get internet, even in the most remote regions, but it is not at the level of North Europe, and there are still parts of Italy with no coverage.

Italians tended to rent property per bed space, with extras on top – sheets, towels, final cleaning, etc. It's much easier to rent at an inclusive price for the whole property – easier on the maths and easier on prospective clients who don't have to do intricate sums to know how much it will cost for the week.

However, if a 3 bed house is booked by only 2 people any discount will reflect the fact that laundry and utilities will cost less – and a management agent wont appreciate them sleeping in different beds each night.

You will also have to decide who you want to rent to. I have Italian clients who won't, under any circumstances, rent to other Italians. Others won't allow French people into their properties. The Brits are universally accepted as they generally leave the house cleaner than when they arrive and they don't complain without good cause.

Under new laws, or rather a clarification of the old laws, any holiday rental in Italy means the tax is payable in Italy as the money is earned here. Gone are the days of being paid in sterling, and declaring it on your UK tax form. This isn't to say that there isn't any reciprocity between the taxmen - if you pay in one country you can deduct it from your tax paid where you live. The problem is that if you pay the tax in Italy you will have to have a commercialista and become au fait with the tax deadlines and laws. You can opt for a cedolare secca- a lower basic rate with no deductions, or pay your theoretical full rate (dependent on your income) and claim deductions for wear and tear, expenses etc.

Any rental over 30 days must be registered at the Tax Office. Any rental contract must now include the catastal details of the house and attach a copy of the APE (Attestazione di

Prestazione Energetica) otherwise it is null and void and you will get a fine. In some parts of the North each holiday property now has a unique reference which must be displayed on all adverts.

From September 2017 a new law on the tax payable on rentals has come into force. The government now requires the tax at a flat rate to be deducted by the agency or portal that takes the booking. As most properties are rented 'in nero' in Italy this is a last ditch attempt to recoup the money due. However, AirBnB and the like are resisting the law saying that it's not their fault if house owners dont pay their tax. At the moment the rules are: 20% of the rent will be withheld by the agency or portal and given to the Exchequer. Obviously for small agents this is a crippling requirement. To have the software and accounting ability to do this requires a certain investment so many smaller agencies have decided to stop renting holiday homes, as they have to pay the tax even if the house owner decides not to. The big movers are slugglishly working their way through the courts fighting the manouvre, which means that the law is being currently ignored.

What are you letting? - The three options open to the home owner are Bed and Breakfast, room for rent, or vacation rental. Each is different and subject to different rules and regulations.

Bed and Breakfast is perfectly legal in Italy, but the rules are laid down by each region - so what is valid in Lazio may not be so in the Veneto, and this is mainly to do with the number of rooms that are available and whether the owner is required to live on site. Some regions require that you live in the property, some that you live within 200m of the address, and some are happy that you live in the same town.

 Universal is the need to provide breakfast included in the price in some shape or form. This can be a slap up breakfast with home made jams and yoghurts sitting round a pool, or it can be a voucher for the local bar. To run a B&B the region may insist that your house has a certificate of agibilità. They can also insist that the owner has done a course on how to handle foodstuffs.

The income is taxable in Italy and must be declared on your 'dichiarazione dei redditi'. You do not need a VAT number unless you have more than one B&B.

Affittacamere: These are rooms for rent within a single structure, and again the Region will supply a list of must haves to qualify - some stipulate cooking facilities, a phone, private washing facilities and so on. Others just want a room with a tv. The amount of rooms is key, otherwise you become a hotel or residence.

Casa Vacanza: The classic vacation rental is of most interest to the property owner in Italy. You have a house which you rent out when you are not using it. The law here, again, depends on your region. It will tell you how many weeks a year you can rent, and what pieces of paper you are required to have to work legally. More and more regions want you to have the certificate of agibilità, though not all. There is a distinction between a casa vacanza as you and I know it and what is called a casa vacanza giuridica. If you own a house which you rent, you are in the first lumping - and here you will need to abide by whatever rules your region and comune think up. If you have 3 or more houses, then you must be the 'giuridica' version, have a VAT number (partita IVA) and run it as a business. Dont call your holiday home a casa vacanza, because the local council will assume it is a casa vacanza (giuridica) and probably send you long letters asking for money.

Paperwork necessary:

Letting out a house which is not up to date with its paperwork is asking for trouble. This applies not only to the house but to any land, swimming pool, etc.

As all the properties are in Italy you are deemed to earn your money in Italy even if your clients pay in USD and never set foot in the bel paese. You pay your tax in Italy. You are also responsible for the collection and payment of the local tourist tax, if there is one. Under the DDL sicurezza of the end of 2018 you are also responsible for telling the authorities within

24 hours of your arrivals, no matter where they come from, and this requires your registration on the police website.

https://alloggiatiweb.poliziadistato.it/PortaleAlloggiati/

This site is now connected to the comune for the paying of tourist tax and the Agenzia dell'Entrate for your income tax - so the possibility of doing one and not the other has vanished.

BUY TO LET - Long term rental

If you can't face washing other peoples' sheets and emptying their waste bins, then buying to let longer term may be for you. Here you have two choices. A property can be let on a contratto transitorio or a contratto libero. The latter is a 4 year contract, you usually let unfurnished and have no responsibility for ordinary maintenance. If you choose this option you can also wave goodbye to re-selling the property with a renter in residence, and still be stung for leaks and maintenance as well as condo costs if its an apartment.

If you opt instead to let under a contratto transitorio, its for a maximum of 18 months. You are still responsible for the taxes (apart from the rubbish tax) and you will still want to put the utilities in the renters name. If you decide that you want rid of your renters - usually because they stop paying rent after a month - you will need to get them to sign a 'sfratto' and go to court. If there are pensioners or minors living the property, the judge will probably not allow you to throw them out until the council has found them a replacement home. You will not get any rent, but be responsible for the property. As you can see, its possibly not the way to go if you just want some easy money.

Down to details.

When you go viewing take a paper and pen as well as the camera. You'd be surprised how many houses blend into a single memory of standing in the middle of a field gazing at a cowshed while the agent is jabbering unintelligibly on his mobile phone. Make notes. It sounds obvious but most people think they'll remember, and they don't. And wear sensible shoes.

Download Google Earth – when you've tired of looking to see if the image shows your car parked outside your house in Lincoln – use it to locate the property. 5km from the sea in estate agents speak is 5km as the crow flies – because he's used Google to measure it. In Sicily it's quite possible that 5km 'linea d'aria' is 20km by road. Short of buying a glider it's the road distance that matters.

Make a checklist – perhaps more important for country properties than a sea side flat, but you will need the same information for each property you see – so find out where the nearest electricity is, whether there's water on site, telephone and who is responsible for the cart track leading up to the gate.

In town make a note of actual room sizes. Sizes are generally 'lordo' – overall - as that is how the house results at the catasto (land registry). A house of 90mq is 90mq from outside corner to outside corner. As its not unusual to have walls up to 80cm thick in parts of Italy, your 90mq is in fact only 60mq of habitable inside space. An agent isn't necessarily being sly by giving your lordo measurement, its accepted practice – your rates, your rubbish tax all result from the catasto measurement so it's a type of shorthand which Italians know and accept. A 90mq house which the agent tells you is 60mq calpestabile has 60mq of liveable space – though this will also include internal walls.

There are various ways and means to measure the overall footprint of a house. When the estate agent passed his exams he would have had to calculate the value of a property and technically balconies count as 25 or 50% of their actual size, stairwells, terraces, all have different percentages. However, in practice most estate agents use the larger measurements when describing a house, and balconies, communal spaces and terraces will usually be on a 1:1 ratio – even though for an exact valuation it's the percentages that count.

Documentation. Your agent should deal with this – if you're using a legal agent, you can relax and not worry – it's his job and he, with the notaio, has an obligation to sort it out for you. If you're using a man who knows a man, ask for as much paper as he can provide, and then ask for more. The indispensable bits are the previous act of purchase, a succession or donation – anything that proves the man who's selling is the legal owner. Of course if you don't have a word of Italian the paper won't help much, but as it all has to be collected and gone through before you can buy the property it's best to start early.

An agent may ask you to sign a piece of paper before you go and see a property. There are two reasons for this. Firstly he needs your consent for the privacy laws, and secondly by signing the agent has the right to his commission in any resulting sale. The Civil Code says the agent has a right to his commission if a sale results from his intervention. The exact intervention is open to interpretation: the agent would see it as he showed you the house, the buyer might view it as submitting a proposta d'aquisto, (a formal offer to buy). The actual dividing line is finer, but basically if the agent showed you a house and you met the owner and subsequently decided to buy, that agent has a right to his commission, even if you then buy privately. Via a different agent not. And even if the sellers mandate with the agent has expired, the agent has a right to his commission for a further year.

Lets be wildly optimistic and assume you find your perfect house on day one. What next?

Your modes of purchase are many and various – the first thing you have to decide is when you want to sign the completion, as everything else bears on that.

There are stories of houses which change hands in 24 hours, but remember – you're in Italy. The minimum time that a simple sale can take will be a week – and that's with everyone working flat out. Much more realistic is a month. Or two. Three if you want to buy in the summer and August falls into the equation. It also depends what you are buying. If there is any land involved with the sale, which is not classed as a pertinence to the property it must have a Certificate of Urban Destination – the famous CDU – certificato di destinazione urbanistica, which tells you everything you can and can't do with the land. This is issued by the commune and takes time to obtain. As it is only valid for one year from the date of issue, it is rare that a seller will have one ready and waiting for a buyer to come along. The seller should pay for this certificate, although there is nothing in writing to force him to do so, but as he cannot sell without it, it's logical that the onus is on him to provide it.

It makes sense doesn't it to find out whether the commune is planning to build a road at the bottom of your garden? Try telling that to a Italian comune. It is virtually impossible to know these things unless you are related to the official responsible. However, some international lawyers make great play of these things, but they too cannot guarantee anything when they do the searches, and the small print will say so.

You can only know what is being planned for the area around your property by asking at the comune if there are already planning applications in the system. There might not be today, but there could be tomorrow. A further check can be made on the PRG for the commune, the piano regolatore comunale – which zones the entire commune into areas of residential, expansion, industrial and so on. All well and good unless you're south of Rome. PRGs should be updated every 10 years. As I said, you will only ever know what is planned if you know someone who knows someone. However, if the seller or estate agent deliberately keeps back information which could affect the property you have recourse in law, to the extent that the seller could have to buy his property back from you.

Renting

Some people, not unreasonably, think that it might be rather spiffing to rent a place for a while to see whether Italy is all it's cracked up to be. In Italy there are three time periods for renting: short term (a few months) temporary (up to 18 months) and long term (up to four years).

Short term rentals: You will have the choice of holiday homes, and that's it. Since most people plan on spending 2 or 3 months getting to know an area, the prices of holiday homes can be prohibitive, especially in the summer. Most homeowners will be reluctant to negotiate a better deal as they earn the same in August as they earn for the rest of the year put together. If you're planning on spending a while eating yourself stupid and looking at some houses, come in the winter, when it will be possible to get a decent rent on an out of season holiday house. Bear in mind that few holiday homes have central heating, so your choice will be reduced, and you will be paying for the electricity and/or the gas bottles and this can add significantly to your rent. You need a registered contract if the let is for more than 30 days - the cost is usually divided between landlord and renter.

Temporary rentals: You will need a contract, which is for a transitory rental, up to 18 months, and only valid for someone who does not already have residence in the comune. Transitory rentals are furnished, and are chosen by owners because the tenant has no 'squatters rights'. Usually bills are put into the renters name for the period of time, and some owners try and make the renter pay the rubbish tax too. You should not pay IMU (rates) if you have a transitory contract, as they are included in your rent. A lot of owners will not want you to take residence in the rented property.

Long term contract: the contratto libero as it is known is the standard rental contract in Italy and is valid for four years, and renewable for a further four. The property is usually unfurnished, (even minus a kitchen), and the renter is obliged to pay for 'ordinary maintenance' while they are resident. Here you can have legal residence, and have many more tenants rights than otherwise. In fact, you can only be asked to leave if the owner sells the house as a 'prima casa' or needs it for a son or daughter to have as their prima casa. Even if this is the case, the owner usually buys off the tenant, often helping them to find a new flat to move into. Rents for long term properties are much lower.

All properties will need a deposit and payment in advance. If you decide to leave before your allotted term you will have to send a registered letter (A/R – raccomandata) giving your dates of leaving, at least 3 months and sometimes 6 months in advance or you can lose your deposit.

Contracts must be registered at the Agenzia dell'Entrate, and usually the letter and lessee pay 50% each. If you don't register the contract, you don't exist. The landlord can change the locks and that is that. If your landlord insists on not registering the contract it's because he doesn't want to pay tax on your rent. The APE or energy classification must also be included in the rental contract as well as the catastal details - on pain of annulment in a new contract.

From 1 Jan 2014 all rent had to be paid using 'traceable means' which in essence means a bonifico or bank transfer. This has since been modified to payments over 999 euros - but will undoubtedly change. Save time and money and pay by bank transfer.

Rent to Buy

For three years now you can opt for Rent to Buy - a contract which is based on a rental contract and a preliminary of sale. You gain possession immediately and pay the rent. After a period of time the renter can decide (but is not obliged) to buy the property, deducting part of the rent paid from the price due.

Example: An apartment for sale at 100.000 euros. The rental is 1000 euro pcm. 500 of these euros are rental, the remaining 500 are a payment on account of the price of sale. After 5 years the renter decides to buy and will pay only 70.000 euros as he has already paid 30000 on account (and 30000 in rent).

It is a contract that is allowed variation within certain parameters, the main one being that the maximum length of the contract is fixed at 10 years.

The risk for the seller is that the renter will not buy at the end of the contract term - but he will have had the house rented and can keep the money paid over. If the renter doesn't pay the rent then you will have the problem of going to law to regain your property.

The problems for the buyer are more fiscal in nature. The preliminary of sale must be transcribed to make sure that there are no nasty surprises further down the line - and this means that the buyer will end up paying the purchase tax twice over, and could have implications on prima casa incentives etc. The rental part of the contract must also be registered at the tax office so means a further cost to consider.

Mortgages - They are not easy to find for non residents or non earners in Italy, but there are a couple of providers who exist virtually solely for this purpose. The big banks will run a mile, but smaller mortgage brokers have understood that there is a valid market for tailor made mortgages. The rules are the same - your maximum mortgage can be 80% of the sum required, but work for a maximum of 60% and you are less likely to be disappointed. You will need a mountain of paperwork to be translated and available for the mortgage lender to pore over. You are still much more likely to be granted a mortgage for a new apartment in the centre of Rome than for a pile of rubble in the countryside.

Part Two

Buying

Paperwork

    Codice Fiscale

    Visure — Catastale

                      Ipotecarie

    Destinazione Urbanistica

    Proposta di Aquisto

    Compromesso Transcription

    Act of Rogito Prelazione

                      Underdeclaration

                      Prima Casa

Buying to Restore

Buying to Build

Buying Off plan

Insurance

Swimming Pools

Paperwork

Codice Fiscale

The essential document to do anything in Italy, the codice fiscale (fiscal code) is the equivalent of a National Insurance number. It is issued by the Agenzia delle Entrate (the tax office) and needs only your presence, your passport and a photocopy of your passport. Some agents make the obtaining of your codice fiscale sound like the search for the arc of the covenant. It isn't, and will probably only take 30 minutes of your life.

Once issued, the CF is valid for life. It is a code of 16 letters and numbers which is unique to you. It is usually made up for three letters of your surname, three letters of your Christian name, the year of birth, a letter, the day of birth, a letter and a 3 digit number for where you were born and a final letter. For example John Smith born on 10 July 1960 might have a codice fiscale that reads: SMT JHN 60 M 10 Z 114 T. Joanna Smith's birthday results as between 40 and 70 – so for a female the 10 July 1960 would be SMT JNN 60 M 50 Z 114 T

The primary reason you need a codice fiscale is to open your bank account. The bank will require the original paper copy. Once you start the buying process your CF will be inserted in all documents related to the purchase.

At the Ufficio delle Entrate (usually open 9 – 12.30 Mon – Fri and a couple of afternoons a week), you need to ask for a form (modello) for your Codice Fiscale – technically a 'modello per attribuzione della codice fiscale' You will also need a ticket from the machine for the same reason which will put you in the queue for the process. Whilst waiting you can fill out your form which looks like this: (there's a full size version in the glossary). You can download it here:

https://www.agenziaentrate.gov.it/portale/documents/20143/278893/modello+cf+AA48_modello+AA4+8.pdf/a8287f7f-abcf-c4f9-b4f7-f038486bc7d6

With Covid rules, most tax offices now permit email application for CF attribution. You must submit a scanned form, passport and a dichiarazione sostituiva di atto notarile, which you can find here:

https://www.agenziaentrate.gov.it/portale/Strumenti/Modelli/Modelli+da+presentare+in+ufficio/

and which must be compiled, with a declaration to the effect that you have never before asked for a codice fiscale. ".. di non aver mai richiesto l'attribuzione del codice fiscale prima di oggi"

You can see that its not brain surgery to complete the form – your surname, name, place of birth, (put EE for province if you were born outside Italy), date of birth and sex.

Your domicile needs to be an Italian address, usually you can put your estate agents' office.

Your residence abroad is your home address – country first, then town then street.

And that's it, bar the signature at the bottom where it says Firma del richiedente.

Ladies, put the name on the form that is on your passport. Don't confuse the issue with maiden names as the system can't take it, and you will be asked for your birth certificate to back up your claim. Italian women don't change their name on marriage, and any name change has to be approved by a government department, so its much easier to get your codice fiscale in the name on your passport.

When you've got your CF, make lots of copies and keep it safe, or you will have to repeat the process from the top, but this time asking for a copy of your codice fiscale as it will already be on the system – (same form, but ticking the 'duplicato' box at the top instead of the 'attribuzione' box).

Persona Fisica versus Persona Giuridica

The vast majority of people want to buy a house as a persona fisica - a physical person - or in English - an individual. Some want to buy through a trust, company or foundation - a persona giuridica. Each has its own codice fiscale, and each has to buy a property in a certain way, primarily a persona giuridica will not only need a Codice Fiscale but also a Partita IVA (VAT number). Whether this means a tax presence in Italy seems to be at the choice of the notary who will be doing the act of sale.

Bear in mind that you will need a fair amount of translation done to satisfy the notary. A company based outside Italy can buy, without having to have a subsidiary registered in Italy. However if you set up a company of three friends, for example, each will have to present to sign a the notary, or provide a Power of Attorney. It isn't enough just for the legal representative to be present. Your taxes both on buying and a subsequent sale are calculated differently, the biggest drawback being that a sale is usually subject to IVA for the buyers, which is calculated on the price paid and not on the rateable value, which can cause a large bill for the buyers. It is important that anyone buying from a company knows their tax liability as it can mean a huge difference in purchase costs.

The Visure

There are two types of visura (extract) that will concern a foreign buyer. The Visure catastale (land registry documents) and the visure ipotecaria (mortgage/debt documents). They are completely different and both essential.

VISURE CATASTALE

The Catastal office has records of every piece of land and every building in Italy. The laws are the same throughout the country with the exception of a Alto Adige and Friuli which still adhere to a particular Napoleonic version of the system. Everywhere else the Catasto provides you with information about the owner, the size, the destination and the classification of every lot or particella of land and every building in every commune.

Each comune has two registers – one for land and one for buildings.

Each register is divided into map sheets (foglios) which follow no logical pattern. On each map sheet is written every particella (literally: particle) – which for land and rural buildings show the legal consistence of each particella, and what the rateable value is. The buildings register is confined to towns and will show an outline and rateable value for each numero civico in the town.

Below is an example of a visura for a piece of land in the

Visura sintetica per immobile
Situazione degli atti informatizzati al 3/05/2008

Dati della richiesta	Comune di SCICLI (Codice: 1535)
	Provincia di RAGUSA
Catasto Terreni	Foglio: 124 Particella: 7

Immobile

N.	DATI IDENTIFICATIVI				DATI CLASSAMENTO					DATI DERIVANTI DA
	Foglio	Particella	Sub	Porz	Qualità Classe	Superficie(m²)	Deduz.	Reddito		
						ha are ca		Dominicale	Agrario	
1	124	7	-	-	SEMIN ARBOR	4 2 19 20		Euro 84,91 L. 164.400	Euro 50,94 L. 98.650	TESTAMENTO OLOGRAFO del 5/11/1986 n. 4443 in atti dal 8/12/1990

INTESTATO

N.	DATI ANAGRAFICI	CODICE FISCALE	DIRITTI E ONERI REALI
1	JOHN SMITH		(1) Proprieta per 1/1

DATI DERIVANTI DA ISTRUMENTO (ATTO PUBBLICO) del 10/1/2002 Nota presentato con Modello Unico n. 1467 3/2003 in atti dal 08/5/2003 Repertorio n. 517 Rogante: EMMOLO IGNAZIO MARIA Sede: SCICLI COMPRAVENDITA

Rilasciata da: **Servizio Telematico**

country: (again the full size version is in the appendix)

It shows the commune, catastal code and province where the land is and the register where it is held.

This is followed by the map sheet (foglio) and the particella (lot) which is in turn followed by a sub particella if existent and a further sub division into a portion (porzione) if necessary. The column 'Qualità Classe' tells you what the land use is according to the Catasto – and it can be everything from inactive, trees, vineyard, olive grove and so on. The number of classe is how good the land is for what it is being used for. The following column tells how big the particella is – in hectares, are and centiare – 10,000, 1,000, and 100 square metres divisions – so a figure of 21920, as in the example, would be 2 hectares, 1920 square metres or 21920 mq in all.

The office of the Catasto then works out a theoretical income from the land – which you will see in the following columns – there are two, dominicale and agrario. The first is for most people, the second for a registered farmer – the value is always lower in the second column. It is on this figure that your rates and taxes are calculated.

The final columns show how the information has come to be in the possession of the Catasto – via an act of sale, a succession, or something much more technical – a variazione which is usually the result of a small plane flying over and seeing what is being grown.

Underneath you see who the land is registered to, their codice fiscale (if you're lucky) and what their registration is, whether as owner, usufruttario, livellario and so on. It also gives their percentage of ownership. Finally it states how this information came to the attention of the catastal office – in this case via an act of sale, with the name of the Notaio who stipulated the act.

A visura for a building is slightly different, and here is another example, (larger version in the appendix)

Again we have the commune, the catastal code, and the province: the foglio and the particella and sub particella – much more common for houses in a town.

The building here is classed as A/4, a casa popolare (not luxury), class 3. Square metrage is lordo, that is outside corner to outside corner – which can make a big difference if your walls are a metre thick. The consistenza is 2.5 rooms – these are not real rooms, but catastal rooms, a room being a useful space of a certain dimension, or a kitchen of any dimension. It is quite possible that a property of 2.5 catastal rooms is in fact a rather spacious 2 bed and 2 bath semi with kitchen/living room and a cantina – but the catasto doesn't make note of that.

From November 2015 the square metrage of the property is also included on the visura, which is not necessarily very accurate, but is now used to calculate your rubbish tax amongst other things. It will give you the overall measurement and a second measurement net of outside space. It is however 'lordo' so from outside corner to outside corner.

The rendita is the theoretical rent you could ask for the property, and it is this catastal value that is the basis for your IMU (council tax/rates), and the taxes and fees due on the property. Each comune does labyrinthine calculations to arrive at a figure that you will pay in tax, and it varies from commune to commune, but basically it is multiplied by 110 or thereabouts.

Again you can see how the information reached the office of the catasto, in this case a modification to the official maps of the zone which probably required various particelle to be renumbered. The person to whom the property is registered is then listed with his quota of the property in the final column.

From the visure you can find out the current owner, the previous owner and all sorts of useful information but the important thing to remember is that VISURE ARE NOT LEGAL DOCUMENTS – they can be and are frequently wrong! Treat them as a guide, but they cannot substitute a notarile document such as an act of sale or a deed of succession. (If you live in the very north of Italy which still has Napoleonic law, this is not the case. In places such as Bolzano and Aosta, the visura is legal proof.)

There are also different types of visure, these above are sintetiche (synthetic) – the simplest form, but you can also ask for a historical visura which will give the history of the property from a certain date with any changes duly recorded. Or you can have one without the intestati which just gives the property details without any danger to the laws of privacy – hence the name John Smith on the visure above.

From 2025 the powers that be are planning to reorganise the Catasto, amending the values to reflect current prices. This already happens if you restore a property. Once the work is completed the architect is obliged to revalue the property, and what had a theoretical rental of 35 euros suddenly leaps to 400 or so, and your IMU goes up to eye watering levels. Prime Minister Draghi has announced that the Catasto will be completely overhauled in 2025 – but it wont affect your bills!

VISURE IPOTECARIE

You will probably never see one of these. When you buy a property, the notaio will automatically run off a visura ipotecaria to see if there are debts on the property. In Italy the debt passes to the new owner, a debt is imposed on the property itself, no matter who owns it. Visure ipotecarie are not cheap – every one is paid for – so the notaio will do as few as possible. Usually they are done a couple of days before the final act of sale, to ensure that the owner hasn't taken out a mortgage on the property just before he sells it. Some international lawyers when convincing you to use their services guarantee to run off more visure – so will the notaio if you ask him, but you will pay him for it.

If the visure come up negative, there is no problem and the sale can go ahead. After all, the seller has promised in the compromesso to sell the property without debt – but in Italy its easy to discover that one of the government agencies has placed a debt on your land without you knowing anything about it. Here they don't send the bailiffs round to take your telly, they mortgage your olive grove instead.

Having a debt on your promised land isn't the end of the world. It just makes the act slightly more complicated – usually with you, the seller and the notaio jogging off to the nearest debt collection agency office to pay off the outstanding balance on the day of the act. Only when that is done will the notaio release the balance of the price paid to the seller.

Certificato Di Destinazione Urbanistica

The Holy Grail of land certificates – it is essential to have before the sale, and impossible to sell without. Released by the commune and a very official document that can technically only be applied for by a 'professional' person (geometra, architect, ingegnere), it tells you exactly what the land is, what you can do with it, and whether there are restrictions and why.

Heres an example:

```
Comune di NOTO
Ufficio Tecnico
Registrazione n. 678/2007
Attestazione C/c postale n. 0137
Data 17/12/2007 Ufficio 60/027 88
Diritti di segreteria €. 51,65
```

ORIGINALE

CITTÀ DI NOTO
PROVINCIA DI SIRACUSA

Ufficio : Tecnico SETTORE 4
GESTIONE E SALVAGUARDIA DEL TERRITORIO
SERVIZIO URBANISTICA

NOTO Lì 18/12/2007

CERTIFICATO DI DESTINAZIONE URBANISTICA
(art. 18 secondo e terzo comma, Legge 28/02/85 n. 47)

IL DIRIGENTE

Vista l'istanza presentata in data 12/12/2007 Prot. 43260 dal Sig. SAETTA Francesco diretta ad ottenere il certificato previsto dall'art.18 della Legge 28/02/85 n. 47, relativamente all'area ubicata nel territorio del Comune di Noto, C.da "Laufi – Battaglia" in catasto al Foglio n° 314 part.lla 186 e al Foglio n° 315 part.lle 63 - 134, così come evidenziato nello stralcio catastale allegato alla istanza;
Visti gli atti d'Ufficio;

CERTIFICA

Che l'area relativa al:
- Foglio n° 314 part.lla 186 ricade in Zona "E" – Agricola;
- Foglio n° 315 part.lle 63 – 134 ricade in Zona "E" – Agricola, del P.R.G. del Comune di Noto approvato dall'Assessorato Regionale Territorio e Ambiente con Decreto n. 334/DRU dell'11/05/1993, pervenuto a questo Comune in data 21/05/1993 prot. n. 12258 e successive modifiche approvate con D. A. n. 634 del 22/11/2001.

Destinazione urbanistica della zona:

CAPO VI - Zone Agricole E

- Art. 30 - Generalità e classificazione delle Zone E.

  1 - Le zone agricole sono destinate all'esercizio dell'agricoltura, intesa non solamente come funzione produttiva, ma anche come funzione di salvaguardia del sistema idrogeologico, del paesaggio agrario e dell'equilibrio ecologico e naturale.

  2 - In queste zone sono consentite abitazioni, e attrezzature necessarie alle attività di cui sopra, nonché impianti o manufatti edilizi destinati alla lavorazione e trasformazione dei prodotti agricoli e zootecnici e allo sfruttamento dei caratteri artigianale di risorse naturali, purché il numero degli addetti non sia superiore a 20 così come previsti dall'art. 22 della legge Regionale 27/12/1978 n. 71.

  In queste zone il P.R.G. si attua per intervento diretto. Le relative concessioni possono essere ottenute, in base alle indicazioni delle presenti norme, unicamente dai proprietari, concedenti o conduttori di licenza, nonché dagli affittuari o dai mezzadri che, ai sensi delle leggi vigenti

hanno rispettivamente acquisito il diritto di sostituirsi al proprietario nella esecuzione delle opere oggetto della licenza stessa.

La richiesta di nuove costruzioni di attrezzatura dovrà essere corredata da una relazione che dimostri la congruità delle dimensioni dei fabbricati e delle loro dimensioni rispetto alle dimensioni delle superfici culturali (in affitto e/o in proprietà, ma comunque nel territorio comunale) dell'azienda ed ai suoi programmi produttivi.
Per i nuovi impianti zootecnici, la superficie colturale deve assicurare almeno il 50% della base alimentare necessaria all'allevamento. Per gli allevamenti suinicolo il progetto dovrà indicare adeguate misure per la depurazione degli scarichi.

3 - Si applicano per queste zone nelle nuove costruzioni i seguenti indici e parametri:
a) indice di fabbricabilità fondiaria:
- per abitazioni mc/mq. 0,03;
b) altezza massima metri 7,50, salvo per volumi tecnici, silos ed affini;
c) distanza minima dai confini metri 10.

Il presente certificato conserva validità per un anno dalla data del suo rilascio salvo che non intervengano modificazioni degli strumenti urbanistici vigenti.

Il Dirigente del Settore
(Ing. G. PAVACCIO)

It shows the commune which releases the certificate with every particella listed.

It will go on to say what the destination of the land is according to the Piano Regolatore of the Comune – for example agricultural land is Class E, and which then has subdivisions as to the type of agricultural land it is. It will go on to say what you can build, how much, and with what restrictions on the land.

Vincoli – literally chains – on the land are listed – by particella and by type. For instance, a particella near a river will have a vincolo idro-geologico – which basically means that you can't build within 150m of a water course. Vincoli of the forestry commission or the Beni Culturali mean that you can build but according to their constraints which can vary from the type of tiles you put on the roof to the distance from a tree. You ignore such vincoli at your peril.

Some communes will then go on to say what and how you can build.

There will be the permitted cubic metrage, and its ratio: for E1 agricultural land the ratio is 0.03mc/mq – that is 3 cubic metres for every 100 square metres that you own. – However, its not that simple. The CDU will go on to say that you can build a church, a school, a small factory where you like, but a house must be a certain height to the gutter line, a certain distance from the boundary, and so on. It can be frustrating, but at least you know where you are legally and what you can do with your land. It can be a useful get out clause to have inserted into the compromesso a phrase such as 'depending on a favourable CDU' which if you discover you can't build on your land annuls the compromesso and you get your money back.

The example above shows that you can build the usual ratio of 0.03mc/mq, (metri cubi/metri quadri) to a maximum height of 7.5 metres and the limit from any boundary must be kept to 10 metres.

Certificato di Conformita Urbanistica.

Most people, Italians included, think that if their house is registered at the Catasto, then that's it. It isn't. The Catasto and the Comune are two distinct entities, and have little to do with each other.

Taking a hypothetical case: I want to buy a house built at the beginning of the 20th century. The owner has provided a catastal plan which is the 'stato di fatto' and a visura, so I know the house is his to sell. What I dont know is whether the work that has obviously been done (lets say a terrace and a mansard) was ever carried out with the approval of the comune. It results on the plans, so technically i cant be accused of having done it myself, but what I now need to do is go to the comune and ask to see the file the urbanistica department holds on my house. A house built in the early 1900s may have nothing at the comune, but lets assume that when the archivist locates said folder, inside there's a permission from the early 1960s allowing the creation of a mansard and a terrace. All well and good, I can now have the certificate of conformita – as the property has followed all the rules. I, armed with my certificate, can buy the house in complete confidence, and even ask for 110% incentives for modernisation works.

What will probably happen, though, is that your search will turn up nothing. This could take various forms – from no folder at all, to a folder with an original building permit and nothing thereafter. Either of these options means no certificate – instead you can have a declaration to the effect of – there is nothing we know about this property since it was built – which will either satisfy your requirements, or not. It will probably give the seller a nervous breakdown as he will have to engage an army of people to sort out the lax record keeping, before the house will be ready for a sale.

Obviously, if the house is a new build or was built after 2000 it must have a certificate of conformity, as is the case with a property which has had extensive building work in the last 20 years.

Bearing in the mind the pre 1967 rules, the fact the no-one asked for permission to do anything unless they really really had to, and the terrible archives of many comunes, its not a given that your request to see your property's documentation will turn up anything. If on the other hand, it does and it turns out that the permission granted was to build a woodshed that has miraculously become a 25mq kitchen, then you're in trouble. Thus begins a race to release backdated paperwork, and pay all the stuff that should have been paid years ago. All possible if you can prove that the house predates 1967. If not, and it was patently built in the 1980s then you have a house that you can neither sell nor buy without doing a bit of demolition first.

Just to throw a spanner sized thing in the works: the Conformita of the building is not necessary to have a certificate of agibilità which comes dependent on hygiene and health and not on the addition of a 3rd floor kitchen.

To get a Certificato of Conformità you need a geometra or other professional who will toddle off to the comune and ask to see the file on your house. He will need a payment of 10 euros or so, and a form signed by you. My comune takes appointments 2 months hence, so it's worth planning well in advance. Once the file has been produced, if all is in order you can ask for the release of the certificate. If not, you will need said geometra to start planning a way through the subsequent maze.

A final word. A certificate of Conformita is not currently obligatory to sell a property, but the buyer has the right to ask for one.

So you've made the offer...

The only essentials in the buying process are the offer and the final act (Rogito). The proposta and the compromesso are optional. If you are doing things by the book, you can do all three – proposta, compromesso and then the act. Or you can miss out the compromesso (usually only advisable if there is a short period of time between the proposta and the act), or the proposta (and go straight to the compromesso).

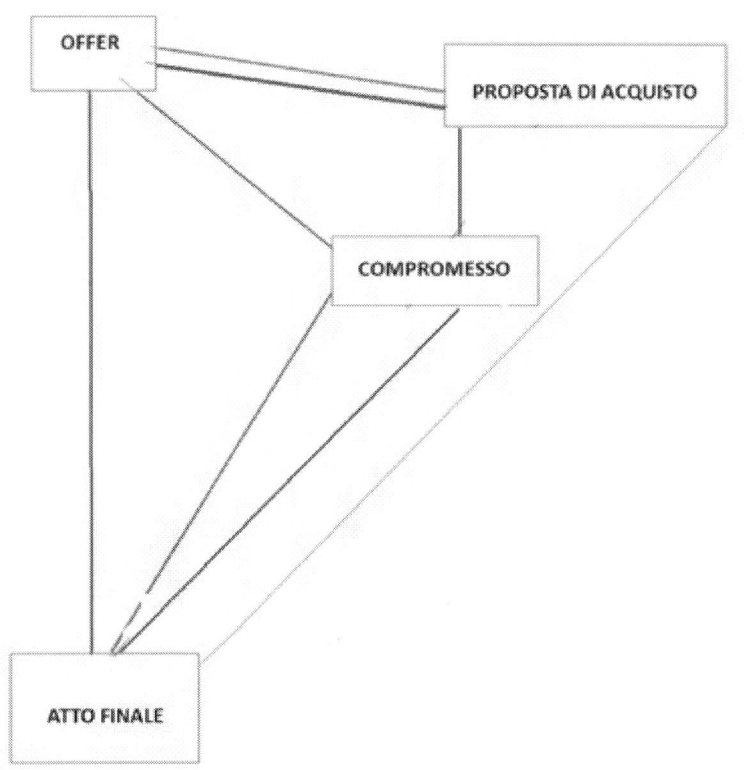

Proposta di Acquisto – proposal to purchase

This is a formal document with a bit of money attached which will take the house off the market while you sort out the next step of the buying process. If you buy through an agent, the money you put down as a deposit shouldn't even change hands – the cheque will sit in the estate agents office. What is important that you show you're serious. However, the deposit you offer at this point is usually a 'caparra confermatoria' so you can lose it, or the seller has to give you double back if he finds a better offer. Usually the 'trattativa' – bargaining will have been done by the time you submit the proposal to purchase and the acceptance is a foregone conclusion. Occasionally they're useful to push the seller in the right direction.

If you write a cheque or leave a bankers' draft for the proposta, make sure it is payable to the seller and NOT the agent, otherwise you have no control over the agent cashing it.

The form is similar to a compromesso, but a proposta is strictly a 'carta privata' – a private contract between you and the seller. It will state who you both are, what you are buying and what is for sale, with a price, a date by which the next step will take place, a date for the final act of sale, and the fact that there is an agent involved.

Usually a proposta di acquisto has an auto-expiry of 7 or 14 days. If you have received no answer by that time, you can assume the owner hasn't signed. If they countersign the proposta it's all systems go, and you need to get moving on the next step of the purchase process. If you don't fulfill your side of the proposta at this point, the estate agent is obliged to hand over your cheque to the seller and you say 'addio' to one or two thousand euros.

Quite a few agents like to pretend a proposta is like a compromesso. The reasons for this are principally a) they dont have to register it so save a morning queuing at the tax office, and b) it isnt registered so they can try and ask for their commission under the table.

However, the tax office has cottoned on to this, and a proposta that is valid for more than a month is not looked kindly on - and may bring fines and sanctions for all and sundry.

Compromesso or Preliminare di Vendità

The second phase of three towards the purchase.

The compromesso is a legally binding document. Even if you change your mind and decide not to buy, lose your deposit and wave a white flag, the seller can go to court to force you to buy. Likewise, you can force the seller to fulfil his side of the bargain – if you have a predilection for spending, Bleak House style, the next ten years of your life sitting in lawyers offices and courtrooms.

The compromesso has a set form — it must include certain information or it is null and void. It must say who the seller is (even if not the owner!) and who the buyer is. It must go on to say what the property is, how much it is being sold for and when the act of sale will take place. It's slightly disconcerting to realize that I can sign a compromesso with someone promising to sell them the Coliseum — and its legally binding. I am obviously not the owner, but the compromesso does not require that I am the owner, only that I oblige myself to sell that property for that sum by that date. Its not entirely surprising that some people sign compromessos and take the money and run.

A sensible person will sign a compromesso at a notaios office or in the office of a legal estate agent. They will not sign it in a bar with a bloke who says the owner has given him the power to sell his house. Since 1 January 2009 it is a legal requirement to register the compromesso at the Ufficio delle Entrate (the tax office), if there is an agent involved. It does give a bit more of a safety net for the buyer and seller, but it costs — usually at the buyer's expense. If it's a standard compromesso it will cost 200 euros, bolli for 16 euros related to the amount of pages, and a percentage of the caparra or deposit. This percentage can be lopped off the tax payable at act, (as long as there are no ifs and buts clauses in the preliminare). At the notaio the compromesso can be either a carta privata (private contract) or a public act, in which case it must be registered and transcribed by the notaio.

Why register the compromesso? – well, it proves it exists and is dated, and more importantly raises a bit of money for the hard pressed state. There is a huge difference between registering a compromesso and transcribing a compromesso, and not only in price.

TRANSCRIPTION:

There are lots of stories floating around of hapless people who sign a compromesso on a property only to find out that the owner has then signed another one the same day with someone else – in fact there's more than one Italian film on the subject. It doesn't happen often, not even rarely nowadays, but occasionally you hear of people being fleeced. Transcribing a compromesso is a legal process, whereby the document is registered with a special office and dated. If there were to be 2 or 3 compromessos for the same property, the one that was transcribed first, is the one with legal precedence. So, Tizio signs a compromesso on 31 July for a house and goes on his holidays transcribing the contract when he comes back on 17th August. In the meantime, on August 5th Caio signs a compromesso and rushes straight off to the office where it is transcribed by August 6th. Even though Tizio was first, Caio has first option of whether to proceed with the purchase. Transcription is not something to get in a tizzy about – I've rarely felt the need to transcribe a compromesso to protect the client, and it costs the same as the final act of sale, so its only worth doing if you really don't trust the seller an inch, or to be truly decimal and European, un centimetro. However, if you have long period between the preliminary and the final act, or you are taking possession of the property prior to the final act, transcribing the compromesso is the only way to protect yourself against someone else arriving on the scene with a suitcase full of cash.

The Compromesso is also the time to insert clauses to protect yourself. If, for example, you are planning on buying using a mortgage – it is essential to insert a 'subject to mortgage offer' clause in the compromesso. In some areas this can prove difficult. The financial markets are way ahead of the old legal systems and writing in a mortgage clause can cause the entire sale to founder. For the seller, the all important compromesso becomes binding only on the seller, all the buyer has to do is ring the notaio and say that the bank has refused his mortgage and he gets his money back. Its just not fair. If there is a subject to… clause its always a good idea to see if the notaio or the agent can hold onto the caparra (deposit) until the suspensive clause has been resolved. If the seller cashes the cheque you may have to go to court to get your deposit back. Get it back you will, but it adds time and more money to an already stressful process.

The compromesso will also say that the seller guarantees and obliges himself to sell the property without debt or burden.

Yeah, right. Look up visure ipotecarie at this point and then talk to your agent or notaio about checking out the seller.

Its not always possible to write the exact date of the final act in the compromesso. What is important to know is that is the <u>last possible</u> date for the act to be signed that you are agreeing. It can always be signed before. So decide when you want to sign the act, and add a month. In 99% of cases if you have postpone the act for a fortnight because there are no flights, or the bank has lost your money there is no problem – most sellers are amenable to slight postponements – we are in Italy after all.

The compromesso includes the caparra – a deposit which is non returnable. It is usually between 20 and 50% of the property price, but can be as low as 10% if you have a nice seller. There are two types of caparra – confermatoria and penitenziale. The former gives you double back if the seller defaults, and the seller can force you to buy or the buyer can force the seller to sell, - the latter just returns your deposit. A Caparra confermatoria is more usual nowadays, but a seller may insist on a caparra penitenziale if the sale is at risk through no fault of their own. If you pull out after the compromesso you lose the money, so fixing a low price can be attractive. However, it also means that if the seller gets a subsequent higher offer for the property it can be economically viable to give you double back and sell to the other guy instead – so putting down a decent deposit protects you as well as the seller.

Finally, as is common in the south of the country, if there are multiple owners it is always safer to get them all to sign the compromesso – or you could end up with a quota of the building and not the whole shebang.

It all sounds alarming, but the vast majority of sellers are honest people who just want to sell their house, and they will be accommodating and helpful in every way they can.

POSSESSION – You can take possession of the property at the point of compromesso, if agreed with the seller. If this is the case the caparra is usually much higher – at least 50% - but if you are working to a tight deadline, or homeless, it can be attractive to gain immediate possession of the property. It is a highly sensible move to transcribe the preliminary if you are taking possession at this point.

According to Italian law and the Codice Civile, the affair is concluded at the point of compromesso, and the act is just a formality. However, with all the possible complications it's best to tread warily.

If you sign a compromesso in an agent's office, it is more than likely that before the ink is dry on the contract, the agent will demand you write him a cheque. As previously said, the civil code regards the preliminary as the sale, and therefore the agent has the right to be paid at this point. Its something I personally dont hold with - but if you want the agent to wait until the act of sale before he is paid, you need to sort it out before hand, and get the agreement in writing. I acted on behalf a client recently with an agency in Siracusa, and the agency demanded that the cheque for the caparra was divided into two - some to the seller and some to the agency, (to pay the sellers commission). I was gobsmacked. As a buyer you have no obligation to do other than pay the seller -in fact for antirecycling its advisable - and I refused point blank. The problem is the agency's, not the buyer's, nor the seller's.

Buying in absentia - is possible, and not too complicated but you must follow the rules.
For those who don't want to spend airfares and holiday time actually buying their property, it is possible to do the whole thing remotely, and could save you money. Having said that, many agents and notaries will have problems.

The procedure would be as follows.
A Power of Attorney - the buyer must stipulate a POA to a third party in Italy to buy on their behalf. This cannot be the agent as there is an obvious conflict of interest, unless the agent is acting solely for you and not taking commission from the seller.
The POA must be a specific POA: an instruction to buy a certain property at a certain price. If the POA is done in your home country it must also have an apostille attached (unless

your local consulate has a notaio who can stipulate the procura in Italian). Then the whole lot must be translated into Italian - either by the issuing office or in Italy at the Court. It is preferable for the notary in Italy to draft the POA so there are no mistakes - some consulates are dire. From personal experience I have had an Italian consulate in America do a POA three times.

Once you have the POA it must be sent to Italy - the notary needs the original for the act of sale, and it will be then attached to the act of sale, so will not be valid for other operations.

The money needs to be sent to cover the expenses and the purchase price. Usually you cannot send money to notaries - they do not hold escrow accounts in Italy, so it will be sent to the POA holder who has a legal obligation at that point to do what you ask.

The Italian state provides for a payment of 6% to a POA holder to act on your behalf, so if its a lawyer they will charge you that percentage of the purchase price of the property they are to buy. An agent should do it for the same fee they would charge you as a purchaser.

The other option is to go to an Italian notary when you are in Italy and have started the purchase. It saves a lot of time, and the notary will then do the act of sale with a POA he has already prepared. As most notaries will ask for a POA anyway if you don't speak Italian, it shouldn't cost you any more but give you leeway as to when and how you sign the act of sale.

You will need a translator and a witness present, but you don't need to have the future POA holder in the room with you.

Act of Rogito – the Completion

Even if you have winged it up to this point with Google translate, the Act of Rogito requires by law that you have a translator if you are not fluent in Italian. It's also in your interest to know what you're signing.

Notaios work in different ways – some want the easiest way out and go home for a nap, others will actually take care of their clients and want what is best for them. Either way, a notaio is independent, works for the state – not you, and is always, always late. I have heard some people say that it took four hours to sign their act – that's no problem believe me. You should be worried if the notaio does it in 10 minutes. There is one notaio I know of who had a record of signing 120 acts in one day. Lots of money for him and no guarantees for the buyer or seller that he had done his job properly.

If you are using a translator, the quickest and usually cheapest option is to sign a procura (power of attorney) for someone else to sign the act on your behalf. It's all done in one go, but the translator only has to translate a relatively short document, you give the procura to someone else, and the act of sale is completed only in Italian.

This is by far the best method if you are going to be having a mortgage granted on the property. The mortgage also requires a notarile act, and they run to 40 odd pages usually – your translation fees would be astronomical. The costs of a procura are between 100 and 200 euros for the notaio, a translator and a witness who speaks English and Italian. They don't have to be Italian citizens, but they must be resident in Italy.

If you would rather have your act in English, the translation fees in Italy are usually 'per page' if it's a written translation, or by the hour if its verbal. Good translators are few and far between in the south – they may well be listed at the Chamber of Commerce – the Camera di Commercio – in the register of experts. Its not a legal requirement for a translator to be registered unless they undertake court translations, but it's a good indicator that at least they will translate what is put in front of them. Some agents can produce a translator – but its not unheard of that they only translate the bits of the documents the agent wants you to know about.

The Act itself is read out loud by the notaio in Italian and by the translator in English – it has a set form like the compromesso and includes all the little details about the property, as well as financial stuff, legal declarations etc. It is this act that becomes your deed. The act of provenance is the essential document to know who is the real owner of the property. A copy is held by the notaio, the conservatoria of beni immobile (the archive of 'immovable goods'), and you can have a copy free of charge just by asking the notaio. Technically the act should be registered straight after the sale – usually it takes a couple of weeks. I have heard of notaios that in the north say it takes 3 months to register an act. This is nonsense. The notaio has a legal obligation to register the act as soon as possible. If he says it will take three months, demand, shout and stamp your feet until it is done. You can then ask the notaio for a copia semplice – a simple copy which you will need to transfer the electricity, apply for residence etc, or a copia conforma – a signed copy – which you need for things like concessione edilizie.

If there is anything you are unsure about while the notaio reads the act, ask It's your last chance. The usual form is:

> The interested parties
>
> What is being sold
>
> How much for and methods of payment
>
> A detailed description of the property
>
> Rights of way, vincoli, anything that affects the property

> Whether you are buying as a prima casa (first house) or not
>
> Certification required for the sale such as CDU, Energy and plant certificates
>
> Declarations that the house is legal and/or built before 1967
>
> Declarations that an agent has or has not been used in the sale.

All of this is signed on oath – if you lie you commit perjury and there are not only heavy fines for you and the seller, but the act can be declared null and you end up with nothing.

1   The interested parties.

The Act opens with the Notaio introducing himself and then lists the sellers, the codici fiscali, residence and anagraphical details. Then it's the turn of the buyers. It will also state whether you are married and the state of your marriage – ie. Whether you have separation or communion of goods. Under Italian law this is important. A British citizen is automatically married with communion of goods, unless stipulated otherwise – so you will be buying in communion in Italy. You have no choice. Even if only one of you sign the act, the property is automatically 50% owned by your spouse. This is especially important if you are claiming prima casa on the purchase. (check under prima casa for more explanation)

2   What is being sold:

A brief description of the property and its address. Since 2011 it is a legal requirement to have a planimetria of the property, which must be up to date and state the property as it is. The notaio must see it, and it must be signed by buyer and seller. The notaio cannot stipulate the act of sale without this planimetria. In Sicily there are thousands of properties that date from pre WWII and have no formal plans deposited at the land registry. The seller must sort out this particular problem at his expense before the date of the atto.

3   Methods of Payment

Under new laws all money going via notaries has to be traceable. You can no longer buy a house in cash, diamonds or camels. It must be cheques only, preferably from an Italian bank. The act will say how much has already been paid at compromesso and how much remains to be paid at act. Photocopies of cheques will be flourished and copied again. The agent needs to keep a register of antirecycling for 10 years after the event, so your cheques and details will all be photocopied for him to put in his filing cabinet. It is usual nowadays to pay bankers drafts at act, and personal cheques at compromesso though there is no hard and fast rule. However, if you want to pay by personal cheque bear in mind that the seller and/or the notaio can insist that the cheque be deposited and cleared before the act takes place. Not the safest thing to do. As in England a personal cheque is merely a promise to pay and not real money. You can also pay by bank transfer, providing a receipt that the money was sent, and the buyer shows the notaio the receipt of the money in his account. There is always the vague possibility that the seller will disappear with all your money, so bankers drafts – assegni circolari – are the safest way to go.

Underdeclaration

A lot of the older books, and some of the newer tomes on buying Italy say 'When in Rome.. ' when it comes to declaring the price of sale. Until a few years ago it was standard practice to underdeclare the purchase price as it was of benefit both to the buyer and the seller.

Since 2008 there is no longer any benefit to the buyer from underdeclaring – in fact it can only bring problems. Since 2008 year the calculation of taxes and fees calculated on the purchase of a property are based on the Catastal value of the house, not the price paid – with the exception of the notaios fee, so as a buyer you save virtually nothing.

If you do decide to underdeclare because the seller pressures you into it, remember that should you sell within five years you will be liable for capital gains tax on the difference between your underdeclared purchase and your declared sale price – which could be a lot of money – and now remains virtually the only reason why any seller asks you to underdeclare.

It is, also, illegal – and carries a large fine and the possibility of an annulled act of sale.

Here's a typical example.

You find a house on the market for 120.000 euros. The seller accepts your offer of 100.000 euros if you underdeclare the sale price at 50.000 euros.

At act you are not going to claim prima casa – so pay 10% of the catastal value of the property in taxes and fees which amounts to, lets say, 2500 euros.

The notaio leaves the room and you hand over 50.000 euros in an envelope to the jubilant owner, and the act records that you paid 50.000 for the house.

A year on, and you decide you want a bigger house and put the house on the market for 130.000 euros. Tizio comes along and offers 115.000 – you accept the offer – 15000 profit in only a year! Then you realize that you technically only paid 50.000 for the property, and selling at 115000 will bring you a profit on paper of 65000 – and a capital gain liability of 13000. You ask the buyer if he'll underdeclare and he says no. (He could also say yes though you have no guarantee that he will do so) Now its not such a good deal – you saved about 500 euros on the notaios fee at the original purchase – and now stand to lose 26 times that amount. If only you hadn't agreed to underdeclare... you decide to pull out of the deal and pay double the proposta d'aquisto caparra back to the purchaser – a net loss of 2000 euros.

A year on and the comune want your house – they're building a new road. The trouble is, you only paid 50.000 for the house, so the comune will pay you 60.000 euros max

Within 18 months your neighbor who is a registered farmer decides to exercise his pre-emption rights, and as you only 'paid' 50.000 euros, he too only has to pay 50.000 euros for your property. You are left with nothing and a net loss of 50 grand.

And so it goes on - it really isn't worth it.

If you see a house and the agent tells you that you will have to underdeclare – nod sagely and say nothing.

Nobody can force you to underdeclare, and worst of all an agent should not be encouraging you to break the law. There is one so called agent near me of scarce morals and scarcer manners who signs compromessos with owners and then *doubles the price before putting the house on his site which promises all the charms of this blessed island. You agree to buy the property at its new price, sign a compromesso with the agent's dad, dog, or wife (which is not terribly legal), pay 50% on deposit and agree to underdeclare the price by 50%. On the day of the act you pay the remaining 50% direct to the original owner and the compromesso makes no appearance in the act of sale. You pay the full amount, the original owner gets less than the value of the property, and the agent of scarce morals but well lined pockets, takes the other 50% pays no tax, no VAT and then has the cheek to charge you commission. I have heard that there are Maltese clients who are ready to take him for a long walk in the country, but a simple denuncia would do the job as effectively, and the Guardia di Finanza wouldn't be short of willing testimony.*

The rule of this is DON'T UNDERDECLARE – its not worth it.

4   Detailed Description of the Property

Particella, folio, size etc are all listed as well as the names of the neighbours, confines, and so on.

5   Rights of way etc

Here any right of 'servitu' on the property is defined. If ENEL have a pylon on your land it will be detailed here, along with the 'vincoli' – for example you can't plant a tree within 3 metres of a buried water pipe. A right of way will be explicitly detailed, whether its for a neighbour, Telecom or for someone to bring his cows to drink in your stream. Rights of way have an natural extinction of 20 years if not used.

PRELAZIONE – *Preemption rights. The law changed a couple of years ago, and the process has been tidied up and the loopholes sorted out. You can only be in danger of someone excercising their pre-emption rights if your neighbour owns his land and is a registered farmer (coltivatore diretto) and is not a pensioner. It works like this. Seller A puts his property on the market for 200.000 euros, the neighbour, a registered farmer says he could be interested, but not at that price. Neighbour two, a retired postman, is very interested. Buyer B comes along and offers 150.000 for the land and seller A accepts. They sign the act of sale and Buyer B has his geometra apply for a concessione edilizia. Along comes Neighbour two and huffs and hahs and says he should have bought the property. Bad luck – there's nothing he can do. Then along comes neighbour one and says he has the right under prelazione to have the land you bought at the price you paid. Now there's nothing you can do, and you are left without anything other than a concession for land you no longer own.*

Its sounds nightmarish but its really very easy to stop. When your offer is accepted the vendor trots round to the neighbours and they sign a piece of paper cancelling their right of prelazione. It's attached to the act. The end.

Any neighbour with the right to buy under prelazione must pay what you paid – (another good reason not to underdeclare the purchase price or they would only have to pay what was the price in the act), and cannot pick and choose which bits of land he wants. Its all or nothing. Prelazione is only valid for land, (or land with buildings on it). You cannot exercise prelazione only for a building.

6   **Prima Casa**

See the separate section below

7   **Certification**

If you are buying land you must have a CDU – a certificate of destinazione urbanistica. From 1 July 2009 you must also have a certificate of the energy efficiency of the property. The notaio can use his discretion – a ruin will not be energy efficient and this will be written into the act. It is also possible for the buyer to negate the requirement for certification and this will also be written into the act. Approved work certificates for central heating etc can also be included at this point.

Attestazione di Prestazione Energetica (APE)

Since August 2013 the seller must provide 2 copies of the APE at the moment of atto. This is the Attestazione di Prestazione Energetica, and is in colour! Not only is it valid for 10 years, but the notaio cannot now stipulate the act of sale without it. If you are buying through an agent, it should already be existent, as the law threatens agents with a sizeable fine if they dont have the certificate at the moment of listing of the property - which is a bit unfair seeing as its the seller's responsibility.

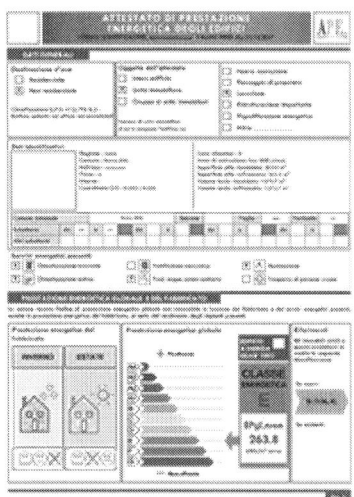

NB - to get the certificate the geometra must also have the catastal planimetria which shows no energy saving structural work has been done. So it's best to get all the paperwork sorted early on in the sale process.

The other certification required for a civil habitation is the certificato di conformità. This is a pretty useless certificate that the seller has to provide. It says that the electrical systems, central heating and water was all installed according to the law WHEN IT WAS DONE. So, if you're buying a house that was built in 1970 all the 'impianti' will not now be legal, but the certificate tells you that they were fantastically legal 40 years ago. It is possible to attach a dichiarazione sostituiva (a substitutive declaration) to the act to make the certificate unnecessary and the seller should oblige himself to notify the relevant authorities.

At this point the floorplans for the property are signed by all in front of the notaio as being a true and accurate version of the property and its 'stato di fatto'. If you sign off on a plan which omits a room, extension or even an internal wall - that is your choice, and there is no comeback should you have future problems. The floorplan cannot be something done by a child in 1930, but must be relatively modern and signed off by a 'professional' to prove that it has been done by someone capable. (Here you may detect the irony in my voice!)

AGIBILITA

The certificate of agibilità, ex abitabilità, ex ex agibilità is obligatory for a new house and anything built since the turn of the century. Beyond that it is not yet obligatory for a seller to provide one unless restorations have been done for which a concessione d'edilizia was required. As alot of people do up a house 'in nero' the agibilità is roundly ignored. My personal feeling is that in the next few years it will become obligatory to provide the certificate at the point of sale, which is going to create mayhem.

To get the certificate you need to prove that the work was done properly, with the requisite permissions and certificates. And it costs - about 1000 to 1500 euros. However, more and more buyers are insisting on it, as it prevents the possibility of nasty surprises further down the line. As things stand the seller is not obliged to accede to a buyers demands, so if you want one, make sure its provision is written into the compromesso as a clause.

If you are planning to open a receptive structure as B&Bs are called, then you must have one in order to get your permissions. More and more banks are insisting on agibilità for anyone who wants a mortgage

8   **Declaration as to the state of the property.**

In Italy it is caveat emptor – you are buying what you have seen and nothing more. If the owner tells you the house is all legal – you need to see the proof. At this point in the act there is a declaration that the house is all as it should be OR that it was built before the great cut off date of 1967, when the law on abusivismo came into force. If your house does not appear on the catasto, or results as being significantly different from what it obviously is, the fact that is was built before 1967 saves your skin. You do have an obligation to put it all in order within a year of purchase.

9   Declaration of agent

As previously said, if you have used an agent declare it. There is a fine of up to 10.000 euros for not doing so, and 15.000 for the agent. The declaration in the act is for the Tax Office to know how much the agent is earning, and whether he is declaring it. It is also important as it is your proof that an agent was used and you therefore have recourse if you have been sold a pup. Writing nothing negates any legal recourse you may have in the event of something going wrong.

Also, if you have to sell within 5 years and have a capital gain to pay on the property, the invoiced amount can be set against your profit. This is also true of the notaios fee and any invoiced work you do on the property before the sale.

When the act has all been read, you sign it. A signature in Italy is not the indecipherable squiggle that most people put on their cheques. A 'firma' must be legible by law, and MUST be the same as that on your passport or ID – that means your full name, no abbreviations and if it has to be written in a childlike scrawl, so be it.

Money and keys change hands, and the sellers usually leave, after which you pay the notaio. His fees are set by law, though there is nothing to stop him giving you a discount. You will also pay the notaio all the taxes and fees due on the purchase. It is up to him to pay the pertinent taxes. Very rarely an incompetent notaio will 'forget', so make sure the notaio gives you a receipt and keep it safe.

From summer 2017, you may need to write two cheques, one for the notary and one for the state, unless the notary pays the tax in advance - ie loans you the money. As the money has to be held in a separate account, the more efficient notaries will simply put the tax amount in a dedicated account the day before the sale, and one cheque to the notary will be sufficient. Some notaries will insist on two cheques, and may well ask for assegni circolari/bankers' drafts.

The act of sale should be registered and transcribed as soon as possible after the act – Again this is the notaio's duty. Once it is done so, the notaio will keep a copy, and this is your 'deed'.

You can ask for a copy either conforma – (signed by the notaio and stamped) or semplice – (a simple photocopy) , and you should hang on to this.

TAXES AND FEES

Your taxes will be calculated before the sale - but everything here depends on what you are buying. A house will have a rateable value and your taxes are calculated on that. A farm building, shed, store or other building that is not a pertinence of a house will impose taxes at 10% of the price paid. Agricultural land calls for 15% of the price paid. Add to this the notaio's fee (see appendix) and the agent's fee and you will leave the notaio's office with the feeling of having been mugged. With the changes in the law, you cannot pay the notaio or the agent in cash. Cheques either personal or circolari can be used to pay the notaio/agent, but only bankers drafts - assegni circolari should be used to pay the seller. You will pay a lump sum to the notaio and he will pay the taxes on your behalf.

What's new ….

The seller and/or the buyer can now ask for the balance of the sale paid at act, is deposited with the notary until the act is transcribed. An act should be transcribed within 30 days - but this is enough time for a lien to be taken on the property in the old owners name. If you have a notary who transcribes the atto in 2 or 3 days it's an unnecessary step in my opinion, but the notary is obliged to do this if requested by one of the parties. If you are buying with a mortgage, it's not such a bad idea, as many banks will not release the mortgage amount until the act is transcribed. In my experience some banks have taken up to 3 months to release the balance to the vendor.

More and more people now choose to pay by bank transfer. How easy this is can depend a lot on the notary. Basically, the procedure should be this: the notary tells you in good time how much money you need for the purchase; balance, tax, notary fees – and you transfer the whole amount to the notary's escrow account. He will charge you for the privilege – in my experience anything between 600 and 900 euros, though the law says they can ask for 1% of the purchase price. Once the act is registered the notary pays the vendor, himself and the taxes. Its an ideal way to do things if you don't have an Italian bank account or are buying in absentia, but there are annoying little problems. If you're buying for 100.000 euros and transfer AUD or GBP to the notary, which arrives as 100.003,47 then your house will cost the latter figure. Do not send less than is required! Notaries are seemingly very reluctant to tell you their escrow account details, which gives a stressful few days trying to make sure the money arrives in time.

A VADEMECUM on buying rural property:

Change of Destination

Depending where you live, the rules regarding a change of destination vary widely. For many buyers the first they know about this is when they find the run down barn and stall that they plan to convert into a rather nice house. Recently there has been a general tidying up of the rules which are now standardised for all of Italy.

For most the biggest problem is the taxes payable at purchase. For a house you will pay your tax based on the rateable value (as first or second house), whereas for a non-house you will pay 10% of the price paid, which can be a huge difference. Many people, buyers and sellers both, have in the past changed the destination of the property prior to the sale, reducing the taxes and allowing work to begin at once. Now the tax offices have tightened up on this, and it's no longer possible. The reasoning behind the move is that if you buy a barn, which miraculously becomes a house with no building concession, you have at best done all the work necessary without any permissions, which can land you in hot water.

Of course, being Italy there is a smudgey zone when talking about hard and fast rules. Many owners reregister their property at the Catasto to avoid paying IMU, so what was a house suddenly becomes a 'unita colabente' which is exempt from some taxes. The problem here is proving it was a house in the past and that a reregistering is possible without the need for a vast pile of documentation. This ultimately is the seller's problem - and it's best to veer on the side of caution. You can always negotiate a discount to cover the cost of the additional tax which isn't your fault.

Furthermore, individual comunes can decide how much they will charge for a CoD, and it varies hugely. Before you fall in love with a cowshed, you need to do your sums, and assume the worst. If you get by in the 'Italian fashion' all well and good, but budget for the need to do things as the Agenzia dell'Entrate would like them done.

Here is a precis of your purchase taxes:

House: a building that is classed as civil habitation and results as A/2 - A/8 - you will pay 2% of the rateable value as prima casa or 9% as a second house. Don't think that to save a few bob you can just declare it as prima casa. If you do, you must transfer your residency within 18 months - with all the costs that that involves - so its not a real saving.

Deposit/Garage/Barn - A C/2 C/6 etc - unless this is classed as a pertinence to the house you are buying your purchase tax is 10% of the price paid for the building.

Unita Colabente - a building which isn't actually anything probably because it has no roof. - 10% of the price paid.

D/10 - a building 'at the service of agricultural land' - 10% of the price paid.

VERIFICHE and RETTIFICHE

Unfortunately, once you have paid the notary and left the office, it doesn't necessarily mean that your worries are over. The state is desperate for money, and each Tax Office now has a special squad whose sole duty is to pore over acts of sale and see if they can squeeze some more money out the sellers and buyers.

If you are buying land, your notary will tell you that the Tax Office has up to two years to make a 'verifica' of the sale. In effect the Tax Office liaises with the Agenzia del Territorio (the agency that handles the catasto), and double checks what you have paid. If the Agencies decide that your sums do not add up, they are within their rights to ask you to pay more. It seems iniquitous, and it is. Forget the free market, the Agencies have decided that property is worth what they say it is worth, and consumer choice doesn't enter into it.

Here's a case study to show what I'm moaning about:

A client of mine bought a property in 2012, a ruin with a couple of hectares of land. The property is in a hugely protected area with an absolute veto on new build, so when we (the agent and the notaio) had to decide values for the land and the buildings we veered on the side of caution and gave the buildings a relatively high value. We got a professional to give a sworn estimate of values and went ahead with the atto. Two years on, the client received a demand from the tax office for 15000 euros. They had decided that the value assigned to the land was too low, and therefore the buyer had to pay the tax due on their assessment and not on that of the notary. The flaws in their logic were pretty self evident - they have to provide proof to offset their demands - and had provided a previous act of sale which showed

1. the sale was a donation from husband to wife (so not necessarily market value)

2. the land was over 5km away, on an asphalted road with sea view, whereas the land my client had bought was 2km down a dirt track, in a gorge and had a river running through it and had no electricity.

3. the previous acts of sale were stipulated when there as a state incentive in Sicily which meant that land was overvalued hugely and buildings completely undervalued.

4. the piece of land provided as evidence was bog standard agricultural land, and therefore buildable. The land subject to my sale was so protected you couldn't even put a rabbit hutch on it without permission.

Once initiated a verifica cannot be cancelled. The moral of the story is that be very, very careful about the values ascribed to land and buildings when you buy; if in any doubt get a sworn document from a professional to back you up, and cross your fingers for the next two years.   (The happy end for my client was that the entire affair was dropped by the tax office when it appeared it had been calculated by someone who was not qualified to do so).

A rettifica is a different, less scary thing - and is pretty common. All too often there is a mistake in a previous act of sale, a typo or a figure that has been copied badly. In these cases the notary can write a rettifica - at the charge of the seller, which sets the record straight.

PRIMA CASA & RESIDENCE

When you buy a property in Italy you have a choice – whether it will be your first house or not. For most people who buy only one property there is little confusion; if however you are buying or have bought more than one the situation becomes more difficult.

You will be asked whether you want to take advantage of prima casa legislation – which in its simplest terms reduces your payments at the act of sale by 7% Its not a huge saving, and frankly, for a holiday home its not really worth the hassle.

If you are buying in communion of goods with your spouse you have 50% of the incentives each, so both of you need to be present to sign the act and get the 100% incentive.

Should you sell the property within a short space of time, you will have 12 months to find another prima casa or you will have to pay back the incentives received.

Capital gains tax is payable on a house bought and sold within 5 years. If you have residency in that house the five years is shortened. You must however have had residency in that property for more than half the time that you have owned it.

> You buy a house on 1 March, and claim for residency on 1 April. You sell the house the following January – you have had the house for 10 months, and residency for 9 months – no capital gain.
>
> You buy a house on 1 March, and apply for residency on 21 August. You sell on 21 January the following year. – you have had the house for nearly 11 months, and residency for only 5 months, - capital gain of 20% on any profit

Should you take advantage of the incentive however, you must apply for residency in the commune within 18 months of the act of sale. Residency is worth the hassle – for lots of reasons – but it is a hassle and is getting more complicated and stressful by the day.

Why take Residency?

Firstly you have to if you have taken prima casa on your purchase.

Secondly – should you want to buy a car you will need it

Thirdly – you get reductions on your electricity, exemption from your Council Tax (unless you've bought a rather imposing palace) but pay more for your rubbish collection.

Fourthly, being a resident allows you a bank account without extortionate charges and you can ask for a credit card.

Must I take residency?

No – if you just want an easy life and don't want to become embroiled in the Italian bureaucratic state, stay a non resident. No one will force you to do it.

Let's get a couple of things very clear at this point. There are two types of residency – anagraphical and fiscal. The latter is the easiest to understand – If you live in Italy and spend more than 183 days a year here, you must have fiscal residency – the UK or Denmark or Canada will cease to be your fiscal residence and all your tax affairs fall under Italian law.

Anagraphical residence has nothing to do with tax treaties – it is merely you saying that your main home in Italy is here, and you spend or want to spend a lot of your time here. However, despite there being differences in law, in practise many comunes make no difference between the two sorts of residency, and therefore you will be assumed to have fiscal residence in Italy.

IVIE - This is a new tax that came into force in 2012 but is backdated to 2011. It is very important to understand this before you think about taking residency. If you take residency to save a few bob IVIE is the reason why you shouldn't. This tax is for all Italian residents and is payable on any property owned overseas. You, as an Italian resident and taxpayer, therefore, have to pay 0.76% of the value of your foreign property to the Italian state every year. For those who have kept a home in the UK or elsewhere, this is reason enough to think very carefully about whether you want to become an Italian resident. IVIE is calculated on the purchase price, the current market price or 'other' depending when the property was bought. Council tax - in the UK - is not deductible as an allowable expense against the IVIE payable. The tax is applicable on private property only - so a house owned by a company or trust is exempt.

Just to add to your woes, there is a further tax payable on any business owned outside Italy - IVAFE - is payable at 0.15% (from 2013) on financial activities outside Italy, and this is meant to include paypal accounts, current accounts etc - with a minimum payable for each of 34 euros. And it's only going to get more complicated.

Let's get a couple of things very clear at this point. There are two types of residency – anagraphical and fiscal. The latter is the easiest to understand – If you live in Italy and spend more than 183 days a year here, you must have fiscal residency – the UK or Denmark or Canada will cease to be your fiscal residence and all your tax affairs fall under Italian law.

So, you've bought your house and you have 18 months to sort out your residency. For EU citizens the following applies:

Comunes differ – they shouldn't but they do – it all depends if someone has read the latest circular from the Home Office. Some communes will demand to see an original of your birth certificate – they wont accept that a UK passport is legal proof of birth, some will want to see marriage certificates, and so on. Legally all that is required is either a requisite E form from your EU country of residence or the following:

    Passport

    Proof of residence – act of purchase, rental contract

    Proof of income – 5,824.91 euros pa for a single person, 8,737.37 for a couple and 14,562.28 for a family of four – this can be self certified – but its still safer to take copies of bank statements, preferably an Italian bank statement.

Proof of private health insurance. You see, they don't want you being a health tourist. Its unlikely in the south of the country, given the parlous state of the hospitals, that even a Brit would think of nipping over to Messina to have a hip replaced, but that's the thinking behind it. So, they want private health insurance for Europe. If you have it from a foreign insurer they should provide an Italian translation of your certificate. It must be valid for at least 6 months from the date of your application for residence. Some regions have now said that assicurazione volontaria – (the state health insurance scheme) is permissible for European citizens, and it can be got from the ASL office. Its cost is a percentage of your income, and is acceptable for claiming residence. Click here for more info, and is valid from 1 Jan to 31 Dec even if you buy it in October.

Birth/Marriage certificates – these should be translated – it doesn't have to be a sworn translation which would cost you a lot, but a decent copy in Italian is required.

Lots of bolli – tax stamps. Of varying amounts. Usually 2 of 16 euros.

Toddle of to the anagrafe office in the local commune armed with your documents and photocopies of them all – Italian offices will not photocopy your documents - and hope for the best.

If you're not an EU citizen (including Brits from 1.1.21) you will need a permesso di soggiorno as well as the rest, and preferably a long term Schengen visa. In the glossary here is a list of the requirements.

If you are eligible for a E106, E120, S1 and so on, take it and things should be easier – above all if you're a pensioner.

If, by some miracle, all goes well on your first trip, you just have to wait for the visit from the local policeman who will ensure that you live where you say you do. Most of the time this is no problem, in a larger town you can have a jobsworth who wants to see if you have a cruet set – that was the total proof required of me in Siracusa that I lived in my flat. When I moved to Modica I explained that I wouldn't be at home in the daytime because I worked and they signed me off there and then – so it does all depend where you live. Once the police have been round, they will take their time in giving you a slip of paper which you will usually have to go ask for. 2 to 3 months is the norm. Armed with your residence you can lash out a further few euros and get a carta d'identità, (identity card) and, if you want, vote in European elections.

Once you have been resident in Italy for five years you can apply for permanent residence, (if you are an EU national) which is now called a Carta di Soggiorno CE or attestazione di residenza permanente.

If you buy using your prima casa benefits and then decide that it's all too much trouble you can trot off to the Tax Office before your 18 months is up and pay the difference in taxes. If you wait and see if they will catch you, you will have pretty substantial fines to pay.

Permesso di Soggiorno

For non EU citizens, the first step to getting residency is a Permesso di Soggiorno, PdS. Technically if you are in Italy for more than 8 days you should apply, though in practice stays for more than 90 days are the norm. The PdS can be applied for at certain post offices – it's a kit which you have to fill in and give back along with a payment for processing. You will receive an appointment for an interview and fingerprinting at some point down the line. See the appendix for the full explanation.

Carta di Soggiorno

For EU citizens once you have been resident in Italy for five years you can apply for permanent residence, which is now called a Carta di Soggiorno CE, although it isn't a carta. It isnt anything - you are probably on a computer somewhere but other than the expiry of your carta d'identita being further in the future you will have nothing tangible to show for it. This should allow you to have a family doctor - but if you are a pensioner or don't pay any contributions in Italy you will still need your S1 from the Work and Pensions office in Newcastle.

For non EU citizens the situation is slightly different – you need to have been in Italy legally for 6 years, that is with a Permesso di Soggiorno, before you can ask for the CdS. There's more in the appendix at the end.

Tax Returns

Even if you are non resident in Italy, if your property has a rateable value of over 500 euros you could be obliged to fill in a tax return (dichiarazione dei redditi) and file it by 16 June every year. As a nonresident you will not be earning (presumably), so the only thing to complete is the details of your property. There will be a minimum of tax to pay on this. Obviously if you let out the property you will be already completing your tax return and declaring your income in Italy - but for those of you who do not rent your house, the Agenzia dell'Entrate will decide that you could do so and tax you accordingly. Even with the new precompiled forms this is not something that is a good idea to do on your own, unless your Italian is very good - mistakes mean fines! It is worth paying an accountant to fill in your form for you. The resulting tax can be paid by F24 from your bank account. However, if you pay a hefty IMU bill it is probable that your payments cancel out any monies due on your tax return. It's probably worth getting a commercialista to give your numbers a beady eye, and then you can rest assured that you won't be getting any nasty surprises down the line.

If your property has a rateable value of less than 500 euros, you don't have to do anything other than pay your IMU,TASI, TARI and other property taxes.

AIRE

In January 2015 there was an addition to the law regarding Italian citizens in the AIRE. A property owned in Italy (assuming there is only one) is now regarded as prima casa unless it is let or given in 'comodato d'uso' if you are a pensioner inscribed in AIRE.   An added bonus for pensioners in AIRE is that any TARI or TASI due is reduced by two thirds.

If you are in the AIRE but are not a pensioner then you must pay IMU/TASI and TARI on your house - even though technically it is a prima casa. However the state assume that you are rich because you work abroad and therefore has decided they want your money.

Buying to Restore

The majority of people who buy in Italy have a plan. It involves finding a beautiful old property with a few acres of land, restoring it for a song and sitting on the terrace with a bottle of Nero d'Avola/Montepulciano/Sangiovese for the next 30 years. Buying to restore however it not necessarily cheap. Locals may not want a stone built hovel in the middle of nowhere, but you will not be the first foreigner with a similar wish list. As I have said before land is worth more than a pile of bricks in Italy, and you will pay market price for land. Accepting this fact you can find what you're looking for. All of this is true unless you want to buy in a place like Tuscany which has strict no newbuild laws. In such cases a few old stones and a catastal record showing that there was a house there can be worth thousands. Conversely, in Tuscany land isn't worth that much, (primarily because you can't build a villetta on it).

People always are shocked by the price of bathrooms in Italy. They are indeed shocking if you are looking at the latest fashion – you can budget 10.000 euros per bathroom if you want the latest designs. At the other end of the scale you can pick up a bog standard bathroom suite for 100 euros if you shop around. Baths are rare – showers are the standard fitting. Similarly tiles can cost the earth, or next to nothing.

Which brings me nicely on to the role of professionals in your restoration. You will need a professional to sort everything out for you. As a rule in Italy an architect, a geometra and an engineer all do the same job as far as residential buildings go – and unless you want a statement building, you will probably be better off with an engineer or a geometra. Don't necessarily take the one flung at you by the agent – there are lots of agents who will sell you the house and restore it – and get rich into the bargain. The word professional is used because they have a letter or two after their name – it doesn't mean that they act professionally – at least in the Northern European sense. You will probably, unless you are very lucky, engage someone who will drive you slowly mad by not a)returning your calls, b) not calling you in the first place c) avoiding you completely d) doing anything humanly possible to avoid doing the job you have contracted them to do. But they'll do it all with a smile and a ready excuse.

With your smattering of Italian and your professionals few words of English you may go far, but unless you're planning to be on the ground for the entire restoration you also would benefit from having someone to represent you on the site. Architects for example only have to visit the site 3 times in 2 weeks according to their code of conduct, which - if there's a problem 10 minutes after they've driven off in their Range rover – means that everyone stops work for three days until they come back again to resolve where the sink should go. Having someone to represent you is valuable – they will fight your corner and not put up with the usual excuses – its called being the occhio del padrone – the eye of the owner – and its not to be underestimated. It is also a not so subtle difference from being a project manager – a trade which, typically in Italy, requires a professional and who is paid as such. With an architect who takes 10% of the budget, and a project manager your costs will rise by 20 – 25% before you've even chosen your roof tiles.

Having got your professional, various builders will be paraded before your eyes – each will prepare a 'preventivo' which, barring 'impreviste' should be the final cost of your works. Except that it isn't.

A preventivo is a detailed written estimate – and is based on a 'computometrico' which is a very detailed list of everything that must be done down to how many bags of cement it will take to lay the floor. Each job and item is detailed and costed. The prices are set by 'the book' – a price list issued by the Region and which details every job in painstaking detail. You should expect a discount on the book price. What it will not include is some materials. For example the tiling of a bathroom is listed by 'mano d'opera' – labour, and by cement and grout, but the tiles are not included as you have yet to choose them. You can learn a lot by reading through a computometrico with a dictionary in one hand and a stiff drink in the other – it details precisely the work that will be carried out on your restoration. Your professional will prepare (or have someone prepare at your expense) the computometrico. The builders then roll up and are given a copy of the computometrico with the prices sometimes blanked out. Bear in mind that for a restoration project the computometrico is valid only as far as the agreed work goes. If there are unforeseen problems, everything is subordinated to the problem (and its expense) being sorted.

Your professional should also sort out the contract with the builders – the 'appalto'. It's becoming the norm to insert a handover date with penalties for late delivery and few builders will refuse to sign one. There will always be a clause, however, 'barring impreviste'. Don't think that big is necessarily best – having a small family firm can be much better than a large faceless 'ditta' with 100 or so employees who send squads out to various building sites.

I have read countless stories of builders who appear one day and then disappear for a month. It seems to me that Tuscany in particular has a big problem with builders. Either that or the authors of a wry look at Italy have no clue about hiring workmen. Most builders start on day one and finish when the house is done. Absenteeism isn't a problem in Italy – work is too precious to be thrown away lightly, unless of course you work in the public sector.

The professional should also sort out all the paperwork for the commune, whether it be a DIA (a denuncia di inizio di attivita –

a sort of nulla osta granted by tacit consent), a SCIA or a concessione, (a formal building licence) or a permit for a well or a swimming pool. Having a locally based professional is worth its weight in gold for this, as he will undoubtedly have a relative, friend or lover who works at the commune to help move things along, and given that each commune releases its own concessione the wait can be agonizing – anything from 3 months to 2 years.

Once released your concessione will stipulate that you must start work within a year and complete it within three, though the latter date is always variable.

The new laws on security in the work place have come as a shock to many – but make sure that the contract states that the building company has sole responsibility for these and their application, and has insurance in the event there is an accident. Your professional will probably be the director of works, and therefore safety is his concern, which if you are planning to do some work yourself becomes difficult as he is responsible for you if you decide to grout your own balustrade. He wont take kindly to you and your friends having a DIY party at the weekend.

The payment of builders and professionals is always a thorny problem. Foreigners are regarded as good customers because they pay on time. Some builders will ask for some money up front to buy materials, hire equipment and so on – and there will be a timetable for other payments, with 10% left until after the collaudo (the signing off of the works). The professional will usually ring you up every time there is a permission to be released by the commune as you will have to pay for it – and they don't come cheap. They are calculated according to the costs of the works you are doing – usually between 3 and 5% of the overall budget, and you have to go and hand over the money before you can start work.

If your property has vincoli or is protected by the Beni Culturali you will have to add a further three to six months to the concessione process, as once approved by the commune, the entire application is forwarded to the appropriate office for their approval.

On the plus side, and there must be one after all the pessimism expressed above, you can set a lot of your restorations costs against tax.

The incentive isn't open for all types of works – but is mainly for preservation and restoration, replacement of structural or sanitary systems and conversions. It also applies for energy efficient heating systems and white goods, so adding a chimney will attract the deduction, as do energy efficient stoves and some pellet stoves both for purchase and installation.

Being Italy you need to furnish vast amounts of paperwork to be eligible for the incentives. As soon as you have your building permit, you need to send a copy, along with your visure, paperwork showing the products conformity to energy efficiency and proof that you've paid your ICI since 1997 (if applicable) to the Tax Office, and then, bizarrely, the health agency (ASL). When it's all finished, you must have paid all your bills by bank transfer, and have a declaration of completion of works, signed off by a 'professional' and have copies of all your invoices. Now, having jumped through many Italian hoops you can settle back in front of your energy efficient real fire and consider how you will ever earn enough to get the deductions from your tax bill.

There are currently incentives of around 60% available for certain types of restoration work, but they are usually tax credits over 10 years - so if you don't earn and pay tax in Italy they are worth nothing. For non-residents there is a reduced rate of VAT/IVA which is reduced from 22% to 10% and in some cases 4% which is not to be sneezed at. See the appendix for the current list.

DIA/SCIA etc

From July 2016 certain works are no longer subject to permissions being granted by the comune.

1. Ordinary maintenance: repair, renewal and substitution of fittings or works to maintain the efficacy of existent (technological) installations.

2. Installation of solar panels or photovoltaics outside the centro storico

3. Works to eliminate 'barriere architettoniche' which do not mean the installation of lifts or works which change the outline of the building.

4. Playgrounds (not businesses) and elements of furnishing in pertinences to buildings.

5. Light structures in the open (also prefabs) such as caravans, camper, mobile homes, boats as well as associated temporary works for touristic structures

The SCIA **is** needed for:

1. Extraordinary maintenance, internal works which affect the structure of the building

2, Restoration and conservative restructuring of structural parts of buildings

3. Restoration 'simple' or 'light' (ie those which do not change the volume or destination of use in the centro storico or change the outline of the listed building).

4. Variants in course of works in a building concession as long as they are not 'essential' and 'necessary for the law'

5. Building works in zones that are classed as low level of seismic risk.

Everything else now takes a CIL or CILA or a full building concession. This is a simplification of existent law. Apparently.

Building your dream house

You've bought your two hectares and now you want to build. If you have 20.000 square metres of agricultural land you can, according to the law, build approximately 200mq of house. As the calculations are done in cubic metrage it may be less, depending on how high you want your rooms but it won't be more. In addition to this notional 200mq you can have the same again underground. Underground is a technical term – as if you build on a hill you can have glass and views on 3 sides, with only one side 'incantinato' and you gain an extra floor. It will never have a certificate of habitation, but if you choose to put a divan and tv in your wine cellar that's your choice. Similarly some people choose to utilize their roof spaces, making a mansard into an extra bedroom. The same conditions apply – it will remain roof space, and if a neighbour denounces you the council will be round with a fine or an ordinance to change your house.

A lot of Italians also use a further agricultural allowance for gaining extra cubature. On your 2 hectares with 200mq of house and 200mq of cantina you can also build 200 mq (or more) of 'fabbricato rurale' for parking your tractor, storing grain and so on – If this fabbricato is connected to the house and becomes a home cinema – be sure to put your tractor in it when the council comes to call.

There are other ways of getting round the planning laws which are all used to the full by enterprising builders – building artisan workspace, houses with a laboratory for processing agricultural products are but two – but its best avoiding them – getting the house sanato (put back on a legal footing) and/or sold is getting increasingly difficult if there is a such a problem with the property.

In a large part of the country the minimum lot of agricultural land to build is now 1 hectare or 10.000 mq. Even 1 metre less and no concession will be granted. However, each commune can interpret the rules as it likes, and in some spots, especially near the sea, lots are much smaller, 5000 or 6000 square metres, or even down to 1000 metres in some areas. Rare exceptions don't have a minimum – but bear in mind if you buy 800mq of land, you can build 8 square metres – which even with the miniscule apartments in London would be pushing it a bit.

TECHNICAL STUFF – the exact metrage for agricultural land is fixed at a national building ratio of 0.03mc/mq – so 1 hectare (10.000 mq) will allow you to build 300 cubic metres. How you choose to do it is your choice, but usually one floor is easiest and cheapest. The CDU will tell you the maximum height allowed to your gutter – a pitched or flat roof is your choice (or the Beni Culturali), so the space in the pitch doesn't qualify as house, but as roof space. Verandahs, pergolas and terraces don't count as buildable space, but they can be subject to other rules, such as distance from the boundary wall. Some comunes do count a verandah – usually it must be less than 20% of your metrage, but it depends whether it is open on 3 sides or less. Some comunes will allow you to enclose a verandah for a set fee (per square metre) but make sure you check before you order your windows.

So, you buy your land – subject to the CDU – and then you need to think about building your dream home. If you know what you want, plump for a geometra or an engineer. If not, it might be time to call in an architect.

Since April 2009 and the earthquake in Aquila the government has made some changes to the rules and regs on building. As usual they have turned out to be reflex laws, and some will be quietly repealed, but at the moment the anti-seismic requirements of new buildings are changing. Foundations now have to be dug deeper, roof beams now must be closer together, and a geologist has to sink more test holes to establish the quality of the terrain before work begins. It all means greater expense for the client, but the situation is in constant flux and by the time your concession comes through, it may well have changed again. Most importantly, it means that having a geologist check out your land is now a requisite, not an option, and will add a few thousand to your costs. Foundations must be deeper than pre-Aquila too, so higher building costs there too. No architect or builder will be able to give you an exact price until the foundations have been built. From that point on there should be no unforeseen problems, and the house should cost what they say it will cost.

Make a book – cut out photos of features and element – but remember to label them. I had one client who produced a wonderful book of 2000 photos and cuttings – nearly all uncompromisingly modern and architectural – and was shocked to the core when the architect produced a 'progetto massimo' of a steel and glass shell. If she had labelled the pictures – ' I love this window' or 'organic shape' – the architect wouldn't have suspected that the resulting building should have been modern and hard instead of an organic Mediterranean style cube. There was also a problem with translation, the architect speaks some English, the client (at that point) very little Italian and its easy, very easy, to get your wires crossed. In these first meetings while you sort out your project is can be worthwhile paying for a translator to make sure you are all singing from the same hymn sheet.

The professional will first produce what's called a 'progetto massimo' which is an almost finished project for your eyes only. From then on, you start paying – first for the progetto esecutivo (the one which is submitted to the commune), then for the calcolista to draw up the computometrico, then for the geologist, and so on.

If you use an architect, their fee structure is set by law – 20% for the progetto esecutivo, 10% for direction of works, 20% for collaudo, and so on. This shouldn't stop you from negotiating.

It will usually take at least 3 months to release your concessione edilizia. From then on it will take at least 1 year to build the house – don't believe estimates of less.

Your involvement is more important towards the end of the project than at the beginning – you will have to choose flooring, sanitary ware, kitchens, heating options and so on. Your input on how to lay foundations is less necessary. If you're not going to be around though, leave clear instructions – 'move the olive tree to here' Don't smash that big stone its going to be my garden table' and so on – otherwise there will be nothing left.

Most builders will want staged payments, as well as one off payments for permissions, big items, and so on – if you're going to be in another country, its worth while leaving signed cheques with a trusted person who will hand them over at the requisite times.

Buying off-plan

Off plan house purchases are still in their infancy in the South, even though Italians from the north are willing to take the plunge. After all the horror stories about Calabria, and disappearing lawyers/building firms/agents etc, it's hardly surprising. Contrary to popular opinion, it's probably better to buy offplan from a small local builder than an amorphous 'ditta' created to sell one particular development.

New laws give a buyer of a new property building guarantees of 10 years, so having a small local builder is probably better if he has to come back because the door sticks or there's a leak.

What's important to remember: make sure that the property will be legal in its entirety – that the whole house will have a certificato di agibilità. It is common for builders to add a room which is technically not on the plans – a bedroom in the roof, a garage which is a living room. If the house will be 100mq then it's important that the plans show a 'civile abitazione' of 100mq. Stipulate in your contract with the builder that the property must be issued with a certificato di agibilità and if it doesn't cover the entire property it is the builder who is liable.

The decree of 20 June 2005 (no 122) is concerned only with buying off plan and it provides a safety net for buyers. The decree requires that by the date of the preliminare the builder (or seller) must have deposited a sum equivalent to the caparra with a bank or insurance company to guarantee all the money that the builder will pocket up until the property is handed over to the buyer. The seller must also provide, by the date of the final act, a 10 year insurance policy which will cover the building for material damage, defective construction, or damage to third parties caused by defective construction which becomes evident after the transfer of the property.

If this is not done, the compromesso is null and void, but can be nullified only by the buyer. All of this is only relevant if the building is still be built, or to be built following the release of a concessione edilizia, but before the completion; ie before you can ask for the certificate of agibilità.

Excluded are buildings which have no concession yet presented to the commune, and those which have already requested the release of the agibilità, and where the 'finiture' have been completed.

House Insurance

Most Italians don't insure their homes. If there's an earthquake the state will pay, eventually, on a prima casa and Renzi promised payouts on second houses too in the earthquakes of 2016. Buildings insurance in Italy is expensive and it is undoubtedly cheaper to use an internet company. As in the UK if you're getting a mortgage you will have to take out insurance via the lender.

Swimming Pools

The plans should be presented to the commune by a professional (architect, engineer or geometra) and there should be no problem if you are within the legal distance from your boundary, depending where you live. (Tuscany now is notoriously difficult to get pool permissions). Opt for a simple rectangle and not mosaics of dolphins.

Good   Bad.

The job is usually split into three – digging the hole, building the pool, and fitting out the vano tecnico (the pump room). The digging can vary in cost hugely if you are on clay or solid rock.

If your pool is to be a surface pool or semi interred you don't need any permission, as it is technically non permanent – but this obviously only applies to a pre-fab pool and not one in cement.

If you have a property with a trivella/well the permission may say that you can't use your domestic water to fill the pool, but you should have a bowser or two to do the job. A tanker of water costs about 50 euros, so its not the end of the world, but most people just fill the pool at night.

There are two types of pools readily available in Italy: prefabricated steel shells from France or Germany, and the typical reinforced concrete version. Architects and geometras are divided on which is best for a seismic area – each has their pro's and con's and ultimately its your choice, though pre-fab pools are noticeably cheaper.

Whether you use a skimmer or an overflow system again is personal choice – though an overflow system is better for a larger pool. The choice of filtration systems is getting bigger, though sand is the base line system.

Natural pools - tried in Puglia and by a couple of hardy souls in Sicily, they're not the best answer, even though they are the most ecological version. The unfortunate fact of life is that the south has too much sun for natural pools and its almost impossible to stop algal blooms. You would need a second pool much, much bigger than the natural pool to keep the filtration up to speed.

If you're going to be renting out your house you must have your pool area secure by means of a closeable gate and fencing/walling to protect children.

If you leave your pool empty in the winter, new laws mean that it must be enclosed by a barrier to stop trespassers falling in and hurting themselves.

Agriturismos and hotels now must have a life guard on duty when the pool is open. Private rented homes at the moment don't have this requirement, but if your pool is more than 1.5m deep it is likely that at some point in not too distant future you will have to add lifeguard to your expenses list.

Part Three

Living

Utilities

Banks

Post Office

Cars and Driving

Car Insurance

Local Taxes

Health

Education

Holidays

Earning a Living

Making a Will

Moving

Utilities

ELECTRICITY

The state owned electricity company is ENEL – and is by far the biggest provider of power in the country. Now the market has been liberalized and there are other providers moving in, Eni perhaps is the second largest. Sorgenia promise electricity from non polluting sources and you save the pollution tax on your bill. ENEL though, being Italian, has decided to complicate things by splitting itself into various companies with the same name.

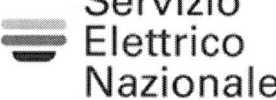

Therefore, ENEL servizio elettrico and ENEL energia are two completely unrelated companies, and if you pay the wrong one by mistake you have about as much chance of a rebate as the Ukraine getting some dosh from Putin. Now Enel servizio elettrico is celebrating its imminent demise with a sprightly new name: Servizio Elettrico Nazionale. Except that they aren't and will phone you continually to try and lure you away to the other provider. From 2022 it will disappear, and if you dont change supplier before the cut off date, you will be assigned a new supplier.

Now, in the heady days of 2022, just plump for ENEL Energia or ENI. If you buy a house that was with SEN, there's been a helpful change in the law which allows you to move companies without having to reinstate the old supplier before moving on. On this basis, you can just get in touch with ENEL – they have an English option on their call centre – and move lock stock and barrel to ENEL Energia. You will need your codice fiscale, the client number of the account and the POD which is the serial number of the electricity meter. You will need an Italian mobile phone number to get texts and an email address to get the contract. Then you can register on the website and opt for email billing and save yourself a few bob. You will get an email asking you for the catastal details of your house. Return the form they ask for or the whole application will go in the bin.

Electricity is expensive in Italy, most of it is imported – and there are big incentives to utilize renewable energy sources, particularly in Sicily where foto voltaics are seen as the way forward.

Aeolic power for domestic use is acceptable, and depending where you live, a small windmill or nowadays a spiral – a sculpturesque double helix which is only a couple of metres high – can be bought and installed with no particular problems. Foto voltaic however attracts the biggest incentives – up to 55% for solar panels and foto voltaic installations, and thanks to the dramatic and swift technological improvements the prices are falling.

The incentives are graded depending where you put your panels – Built into the fabric of the property – ie the roof, you get the maximum incentive, which diminishes the further from the house you put the panels. For domestic use there are remarkably few obstacles for such an installation unless you live in the centro storico of a UNESCO town centre. The Beni Culturali can now insist that panels are into the roof itself and cannot just sit on top. If you take the incentives you can't have an in/out meter and sell the excess to the ENEL however. They will just take your excess gratis. So, for a house that won't be inhabited all year round it can be a better investment to pay up and get an in/out meter. You get free power while you are in residence, and for the rest of the year you earn from Enel by selling on what you produce. The sums are more difficult if you are not living in Italy and don't pay IRPEF (Italian income tax). All incentives are given as discounts on your tax bill, hence if you don't pay tax, you don't get the incentive. Now there are companies who ask for no money from the client, but pocket the incentives and the payments from selling the electricity for the first 12 years of the panels life. You get free electricity, and after 12 years you also get the incentives (they are paid for 20 years). If money is short after an expensive restoration, this is a tempting way to go.

Solar panels for hot water are much cheaper and much more ugly. A standard panel will have a 120 litre hot water tank, which will provide all the hot water you need during the summer. In the winter you will need to top up with electricity. For me it's a bit of a waste of time. I have a 1000 litre plastic water tank above the house and a 5000 litre tank below. Both get the sun and in summer the cold water from these 'serbatoi' is hotter than the hot.

When you buy a house and take on the electricity account you will be asked what kilowattage you want. Unlike in the UK, each contract is for a specific amount or potenza – and ranges from 3 to 10Kw for a domestic supply. The more your contract is for, the more you pay. 3kw will do for a little flat in town, 4.5 for a larger flat and 6 or above if you have a country place with a pool. It's a fact of life that you get very used to turning off appliances before you turn on others. I have a kettle, being a Brit who needs a decent cup of tea, and that's 2000 watts. The hot water tank is 1500, a hairdryer 1000 and the washer 2000 while its heating up the water (all washers are cold water feed only though 'piano piano' this is changing, and the new washing machines also have hot water feeds). Its obvious then, that I cant have them all on at once – or the meter will trip and I have go outside and reset it, then spend 10 minutes reprogramming the tv, aircon, alarm and so on.

Bills are sent every two months, and with the modern meters are read telematically – with a minimum charge, so if the house is empty over the winter, you will have one bill that seems very high for an unoccupied house followed by two where there is nothing to pay.

The ENEL website is a dream, and bilingual, but as in a dream it never seems to do what you ask it to do. Try changing your user date, method of payment, contract etc and it will be unable to cope with your request and you will always be driven to call ENEL on their freephone number 800900860 and ask them to do it for you.

Pylons are the great bugbear of many house buyers in Italy. They have been thrown up with no regard for the countryside, views or houses – and there they stay. There is monophase and threephase, so its quite possible to have pylons of different voltages crisscrossing your property for no particular reason. Fortunately it is now possible to have these moved, or put underground, but always at your expense. Ring ENEL and they will send an engineer who will report back to the powers that be who will send you a preventivo for the work. You can move all monophase, and medium voltage pylons and cables. High voltage (20000 volts and above) with the classic Audenesque pylons striding across the countryside cannot be moved

Should you require electricity to be brought to your property, ENEL will bring it to the boundary, and you are responsible from thereon in. There are bands of charges depending on distance and again, ENEL will send someone round to give you a preventive of the cost. Once you have your estimate you can go ahead, unless of course the electricity supply will have to cross someone else's property. At this point you will have to go and smooth talk the neighbour and find out if he is willing to let your powerlines cross his property. There will be eyes cast to heaven, tutting and sighs followed by an astronomical figure that the neighbour wants you to pay him for his consent. Dont get angry, Negotiate. Without his consent you will be trying to cook and filter your pool with an old car battery for the next ten years. The neighbour holds all the cards, and he knows it. Some neighbours will expect you to pay them for the privilege, others will have no problem as it increases the value of their land, and some will just say no. If it's the latter, you have a problem and need to start investigating the costs of being offgrid. Some people are adamant that ENEL has an obligation to connect you. They are sadly mistaken. ENEL will connect you if they can be bothered. If you need a line to cross a river, a railway etc, it is highly possible that they will refuse.

GAS

Mains gas or metano is not common outside of large cities and towns, and even less so in the south. Even then, the process of laying a gas main in town is teethgrindingly slow and many of the sub contracting companies will wait for a request for connection before they will even consider it. Once connected life gets easier. Gas is not much cheaper than electricity, but for those who want radiators instead of a rush of ineffectual hot air, it's the way to go.

Outside the main towns you will need the traditional 'bombole' which only really work for cooking. A central heating boiler will use up to 2 big ones a week in winter – that's about 35 euros a week.

Alternatively get a bombolone – a larger 500 or 1000 litre tank which will be provided and installed by your local LPG (GPL) or butane supplier. It must be 7 metres from the house, and usually less than 30 metres from a road. Under new legislation it must be fenced, protected and visible. The bombolone is provided free by the gas company in 'comodato uso' – change suppliers and they want their bombolone back. The fire department will have to make a site visit to check your connections before you can turn it on. Boilers must now be only placed on an outside wall of a property – usually in a metal locker type thing which stops the pilot light being blown out in a high wind, (unless its a ultra modern instant version). If you have a boiler with 'camera stagno' it can still be installed indoors. You must also have fire extinguishers provided by your gas company, and your boiler must be serviced annually by law.

To complicate life even further, new laws mean that the water that drains or drips from your boiler (when fitted from 2020 onwards) must go straight into the sewer via a sealed pipe, which is a real pain if your boiler is miles from your main drain/septic tank

From 2017 condominium dwellers must have individual thermostats on every radiator and a meter (if its a centralised system) showing individual consumption.

WOOD AND PELLETTS

Wood burning stoves, water boilers and 'scaldabagni' still sell well in Italy, above all in the south. The designs seems antiquated but they function remarkably well - The Chinese 'antique' ones in cast iron (ghisa) are also cheap – 250 euros but they aren't energy efficient. For a decent wood burning stove you are looking to spend 600 euros plus. A pellet stove will cost from 1600 euros upwards. Pelletts are increasingly available in the south and more and more DIY shops are selling them – but again, they're not cheap.

OTHER FORMS OF HEATING

The new fan assisted liquid gas heaters are useful. They cost from 150 euros and take the vapourless, odourless, 'safe' liquid gas – they have timers and thermostats and come in all ranges of sizes to heat one room or an entire barn. And they work. Instantly. The gas isn't cheap – 20 litres costs about 50 euros – but it will last 3 or 4 weeks in the depths of winter.

OPEN FIRES

An open fire warms the cockles and chimney stack, but little else. Mantelpieces and fire surrounds sell well – they're very English! – and lots of flats have a fake Georgian fireplace with some plastic flowers in it. Actual working fires are rare, but there's nothing to stop you putting one in, unless you live in a town centre or a condominium. The classic back boiler system – termo camino is becoming popular, and not only will it heat your water but warm your radiators and even underfloor heating too. There is a tendency to build an open fire on a shelf about 60cm from the floor, which allows you to look at the flames, but leaves you with very cold feet.

UNDER FLOOR heating is relatively new and the consensus is, it's good, but depends entirely on your choice of flooring. The very swish catalogues also offer underfloor cooling systems, but you pay your money and you take your choice.

GEO THERMAL electricity is very new, and the plants that are existent are generally the work of foreigners who have come to live in Italy. I've read of geo thermal techniques being used in Umbria and Liguria, but south of Rome you'd be hard pushed to find a heating engineer who could even spell it, let alone fit it.

AIR CONDITIONING – hot/cold is the favoured system of many southern Italians. Since the A/C cold costs more than hot, it's best to find an efficient air conditioner for the summer months. Prices vary hugely; you can pick up a 9000btu Chinese system for under 300 euros in a hypermarket, but you will pay 1200 euros or more for a similar 'recognised' brand that is energy efficient (AA). The cheaper versions tend to be classed as A for A/c cold and C for A/c hot. You should look for one with gas type 210 and not 207. The most common 'off the shelf' sizes are 9000 or 12000 BTU and for most rooms they are ample. You can find a simple calculator at http://www.goodhousekeeping.com/home/air-conditioner-calculator

In some centro storicos standard A/C external fan units are now not allowed and you have to have an internal only system with just a small hole for the air intake. These cost much more than a standard system (over 2000 euros each).

In 2019 the rules all changed for fitting and removing a/c units. From September, if you are replacing aircon, you now have to pay up to 800 euros to collect the gas and dispose of your old unit safely. Prices for fitting new units will go up due to the checks the installer must now make on inert gases etc.(about 300 euros a time) Any unit that is hot/cold must have a libretto, regular servicing and so on.

All installers must be 'abilitato' and notify all gas emissions, and all sellers of gas for a/c units must have full traceability for their products.

WATER

Water is one of the main preoccupations for people buying in Italy but it does all depend on where you buy. In some areas the supply has been privatised, in others not. Whether private or public there is a huge difference between what you will have in the UK and what is available in Italy, in quality, supply and pressure. In the north the cities have reliable mains water supplies as in other countries.

Towns have mains water, but many towns only open the supplies in the mornings. This means that you must have a serbatoio or water tank in your property. Usually a 500 litre tank is adequate for a town house, and ideally it sits on the roof giving you at least a gravity feed if the electricity fails.

In some towns the water pressure is pitiful and you need a pump to fill the serbatoio – if this is the case you will have an 'auto-pescante' – a pump which goes in search of water. From the outlet of the serbatoio you will need a normal pump to give you a decent water pressure for the house – and – if you don't want the pump to turn on every time you open a tap – a press control which stabilizes the pressure of the system. As you pay for water by cubic metre its essential you have a timer or ballcock on your serbatoio to avoid losing lots of precious liquid because you forget you've turned on the pump.

Outside the towns the situation is very different. Some areas have a local consortium which supplies water. The consorzio has an artesian well, and pipe water to their customers. The customers own an infinitesimal share of the well, and pay each time the water is turned on. Other areas have mains water from a private company or consortium where your standing charges will provide a yearly minimum – about 180 cubic metres – and then you pay per litre for everything in excess. Failing that you will have a rainwater cistern, which is refilled by a bowser when it runs dry.

The ideal solution in the country is to have a well, or pozzo. A drilled well is called a trivella – and needs a permission from the commune/genio civile to be sunk. An existing pozzo can be 'repristinato' (restored) without a permission, but not deepened though in reality nobody actually checks.

Pozzi for agricultural use are becoming more and more difficult to gain permissions. This is usually because they 'pull' a lot of water – some wells pull more than 30 litres a second. For domestic use the limit is half or 1 litre a second, which is ample and more than you will ever use. Another reason why agricultural wells are becoming more difficult to sink is that it was the classic way to build an 'abusive' house. Get a pozzo for agricultural use, then get electricity to power the pump – and hey presto, any resulting house had all mod-cons. Nowadays, ENEL will be wary about giving a connection for an agricultural trivella if the owner is a foreigner here on holiday. And rightly so.

A domestic trivella will use a mono-phase pump, which also saves on the electricity costs.

There remains the 64000 euro question, however. How deep do you have to sink a well? Again its relative. You might well find water at 60 metres, but it wont be guaranteed. At 90 metres may well be another source, but it could well be full of sulphur and usable only for watering the garden. For a constant supply of good water you may have to go to 200 metres or more.

The actual costs of sinking the well are not huge. About 10 euros per metre. What costs is the sleeve, the incamiciatura. If you're lucky you can use PVC – about 10 euros per metre, but more usually in a seismic area you need to use steel – which costs about 55 euros per metre – and its here that the costs mount. It all depends where you hit rock. The first 20 metres are sleeved – and if after 20 metres you hit solid rock, you're laughing. If you have 180 metres of clay, you're not. The sleeve is used only until you hit solid rock so its impossible to know how much your trivella will cost until its sunk. A good geologist is essential when planning a trivella. Add to all this, 2000 euros for a good pump and you can get an idea of how much your well will cost.

SEWAGE

If you're attached to the mains system you will pay a sewage quota on your water bills. If not things can become complicated. Unless you live right next to a river, lake or the sea most comunes will now want you to fit a fosse imhoff a perdere - a septic tank which drains. These are usually two chamber versions, but each comune can decide on its own rules, and many now insist on a three chamber pozzo. Depending on your location or proximity to the neighbours, the commune can also stipulate a microfiltration system to not let 'acqua nera' seep into your neighbours lawn.

The size of the tank depends on the amount of people using it. The ones made out of cement rings can be adjusted easily in size, the plastic ones not. If you buy a 3 bed house, then you must have a tank for at least 6 people. Better to have one for 10.

The fitting requires a 'pratica' done by a professional with the appropriate stamps from the genio civile, and a renewal fee every 2 or 3 or 4 years which shows you have had it emptied (spurgo) by a registered company.

TELEPHONE

Telecom Italia is the privatized state service and all the other companies subcontract to TI engineers. Since privatization the company has become almost reliable, a line will be connected within 15 days or 30 in the country. The options are now many and various, as the mobile phone companies have made great inroads into the market. In the towns and cities super fast fibre optic is now commonplace thanks to European funding.

The main bugbear with Telecom Italia was that you paid a high standing charge – 20 euros a month just for having a line. Now TIM has introduced charges without a 'canone' (line rental) and is in direct competition with Vodafone, Fastweb and all the other providers.

The WIMAX system is slowly being rolled out, which could make life much easier for everyone who lives in the countryside. As yet, there are few companies who offer wimax, Mandarin in Sicily and ariadsl in Umbria are perhaps the two biggest, but Basilicata, parts of Puglia and Campania are also covered.

The main challenger to Telecom Italia is Vodafone – they offer an instant plug in box, an internet key and fixed line phone numbers – all riding on the Telecom Italia lines. It means that if you don't have a fixed line you can use the internet dongle instead.

Fastweb offers fixed lines, internet, TV down the phone line and integrated mobile phones. Its not the cheapest but is very reliable. The customer service is quite possibly the worst ever encountered.

WindTre is another big player, and there are a host of others.

MOBILES

Vodafone, TIM (Telecom Italia Mobile), WindTre and Iliad are the big four. In my part of Sicily the Vodafone coverage is rubbish, and everyone has TIM. It all depends where you are. Ask around before you buy to see which is the best for your area. 3 is undoubtedly the bargain, but you need UMTS coverage, otherwise it rides on TIM signals. UMTS is around in towns, non-existent in the countryside.

For tablets - all the providers offer a data only SIM card which will give you lots of Gb a month for 10 euros, or thereabouts. You can have pay as you go - which you can't in the UK, so it's easy. If you don't recharge your SIM for 6 months/a year they die a natural death and its back to square one.

To buy a SIM card you need a codice fiscale – if you don't have one the shop which sells you the SIM will generate one for you. This is fine for shopping purposes, but it doesn't mean that the code you get will be the definitive one for you. It all depends if there is another Jane Wilson born in Dumfries on the 3 May 1953 already with a codice fiscale in Italy. If so – the computer at the tax office will generate a different one for you.

TELEVISION

Italian TV is terrible. Everyone knows how dire it is, but don't think you can get UK tv on Sky Italia. UK Sky is available (illegally), but even they are changing the transmission method and some channels are now not pickupable as I believe the technical term to be.

The RAI channels are supposedly independent, Channel 4 5 and 6 all being Berlusconi's private kingdom. All terrestrial broadcasting is now only digital, so you will have to buy a box or a digital telly. The freeview boxes are widely available and offer an extra 20 or so equally dismal channels.

Netflix exists, as do other options including free ones. We are now in the midst of dvb2 and digital tv is being upgraded. If you don't have a tv made after 2016 you may have to buy a set top box or something to obtain HD tv.

The other options are Mediaset Digital – pay TV which has lots of dubbed soap operas and films or Sky which has lots of the same, plus National Geographic, Discovery, and original language options for films and docs.

Brexit has brought woes to SKY UK subscribers who cannot now download their programmes while in Europe. You will have download an entire series and bring it with you.

Various apps will work with a VPN such as Transponder which lets you watch all sorts of non Italian tv for a monthly fee.

The TV Licence (Canone RAI) is now included in your electricity bill. The canone can be only paid once, and will be charged to the property where the owner has residence. If you are non-resident in Italy and have a non-resident electricity tariff you should not be asked for payment. The payment of the canone covers all your properties, second homes, offices etc. If you are a resident but do not have an electrical device that is capable of receiving a signal you can make an online declaration to opt out of the billing. This must be done annually. To opt in to the system, ie a nonresident who does have a television, is much more difficult.

You can speak to your electricity provider about exemption or complete the necessary form and send it to RAI. here:

http://www.canone.rai.it/dl/docs/1461319325886Dich_sost_TV_mod.pdf .

It now seems that Brussels has decided that it's not European to pay your licence fee along with your leccy bill so Italy has its marching orders to stop and invent a new way to pay for Rai's huge budget. No doubt there will be some ideas thrown around in 2022.

RADIO

Not even worth turning on frankly – you're much better off getting on the internet and getting the Today programme through the computer. If you want tv too you'll be hunting for a clever little programme called expat shield, which will fool the streaming providers into thinking you are in the UK and allow you to download, something which I could never advise!

BANKS

Your estate agent will probably recommend a bank for you – don't dismiss it out of hand, thinking the worst. There's probably a good reason. He may have other foreign clients already with accounts there so the mysteries of international non resident money transfers won't come as a complete shock to Isabella, who is more used to ringing up clients telling them they're overdrawn. Or perhaps there's someone in the bank that speaks English, as is increasingly the case.

There are innumerable little banks, but I'd plump for one of the bigger ones, excluding the Monte dei Paschi. Unicredit is in dire straits but too big to fail. Certainly there is no common policy. The bank I use will give a non resident a cheque book and a bancomat card. I have clients with other banks who have not only been refused a simple cheque book, but also refused international transfers.

If you open a non residents account the charges will be higher than a residents account. Banking is not cheap in Italy – you pay for everything, every counter transaction, every cheque, every ATM withdrawal, plus they may charge for receiving money from abroad, as well as the myriad of taxes and fees which get levied with alarming regularity. If you are dead against paying for these services, but an avid fan of standing in queues Id say open an Banca Poste account. They are cheaper and they pay infinitesimal interest on a current account – the downside is that to pay in a cheque takes two days of standing in a non-moving queue.

Bureaucratically there are incredibly stupid rules in Italian banks. You cant transfer an account from one branch to another. You have to close it and then rush to your new branch and open another one. When you switch from a non residents account to a residents account they have to close one completely and then open a new one.

Opening your first bank account will entail your presence. Antiriciclaggio (anti-money laundering) means that a bank account can only be opened in person, unless you're related to the bank manager. You will need your passport and the original copy of your codice fiscale. An Italian address is useful. If they offer internet banking grab it, and then ask for no paper statements as they charge 2.50 for each letter they send you, and as they send you a statement each time you spend any money you can build up a healthy charge. Slowly the major banks are rolling out the internet banking sites in English.

If you go overdrawn they will ring you up and tell you to get along to the bank sharpish.

Now purchases over 1000 euros cannot be made in cash, you must use traceable means - cheque or bancomat/credit card. However, as a tourist (and providing passport) you can pay in cash. Visitors to Italy can bring in 10.000 euros each in cash, without having to make a declaration as to its use. Bank transfers to Italy must contain a 'causale' or a description of what the money is destined for.   In a couple of years, 1000 euros will be the maximum cash transaction permitted.

Because pensions are now paid direct to current accounts, the banks have been told to not charge for bank accounts that hold a median of less than 5000 euros pa. This will also exempt you from the quarterly bollo of 8 euros.

You can open a bank account in Italy even if you are non resident –

Banks do not act uniformly in regard to the type of account available. Some offer accounts which allow you to do virtually nothing, while others give you all the bells and whistles you expect from an account.

A non resident bank account will cost you more than a resident's bank account – usually each operation is paid for, and you will also pay quarterly tax for the privilege. It will cost you at least 100 euros pa to have an account and not use it.

How to go about it:

You cannot open an account online or by third party. You must be present physically to open an account. You will also need an Italian phone number to activate the account, otherwise you won't get online or phone banking. Some banks will not send mail to a foreign address, so an Italian address is useful.

Nearly all non resident accounts will give you an ATM card – (bancomat), and online banking.

Some will let you have a cheque book – crossed cheques only. Remember that cheques in Italy do not have an expiry date and can be presented at any time, so unused or cancelled cheques must be returned to the bank to be deleted. You cannot bounce cheques in Italy.

Resident accounts can have a credit card – but they're more like charge cards. The amount is cleared automatically every month from your account.

All accounts can have direct debits on them – RID – useful for utility payments.

Some accounts will allow you to pay F24 – a precompiled form for paying IMU and payments to the state.

If you dont want a full bank account you can often find prepaid cards with their own IBAN code which allow you to credit money, buy online, pay bills etc and which usually cost nothing or 10 euros per year.

To open any sort of account you will need:

your passport or other valid ID

Your codice fiscale – official version - not something downloaded from the web. It is likely you will also need your NI number or tax code from your home country as nowadays there are cross border controls.

An Italian phone number – now essential as most banks now use 2 stage security to access online banking which necessitate an sms with a code or a certificate downloaded onto your phone.

There are now prepaid/debit online accounts available to non-residents which can give you an Italian or European IBAN and this may be the easiest option. However, post Brexit it looks like receiving banking services from a European bank while resident in the UK is problematic. In fact some British banks are closing their Italian residents bank accounts, as cross border banking is going to be impossible for most banks unless they open a new bank in each European country after Brexit.

USA - IRS and Italian Banks:

American citizens are having some serious problems when they want to bring money out of the US. This is down to the Foreign Accounts Taxation Compliance Act (FATCA) which was designed to clamp down on tax evasion, by giving the IRS huge powers to nose about in other banks' business. The effect of this is that many European banks now don't want to have anything to do with American customers. If the IRS find one example of tax evasion by a US citizen they can virtually close down the bank's operations in the USA and take millions in fines. The upshot of this is that some US citizens find that the only solution at present is to renounce their US citizenship, which is a drastic measure to have some euros to hand when they need to pay bills. Even clients who have existing accounts in Italian banks now are finding that their American banks have decided not to work with the foreign banks, and therefore cannot transfer money. What is going to happen to resolve this situation is anyone's guess. At the moment it looks like it's here to stay.

POST OFFICE

A working knowledge of the PO is essential to life in Italy. Internet payments are still in their early days and any payments to state offices require deposits to a current account that can only be paid at the PO. By March 2010 you should have been able to pay all bills online. I say no more.

You will need a deposit form 'a modello' for a current account. It is in three parts – one big, two small and all have to be filled in identically. You use this modello for paying Water rates, Rubbish tax, fines, fees for the CCIAA, etc etc etc . Its called a bollettino postale, and requires that you queue up at the PO for one to fill in, or find one online:

 https://www.bollettinoonline.it/ fill in the details and print it off to take with you with to the PO.

You can also pay phone bills, electricity bills and so on at the PO – they will charge you for the privilege, though nowadays you can also pay at most tobacconists too.

The postal system in Italy is famously unreliable – you will resort to sending any local mail by raccomandata (registered) and any official mail by raccomandata A/R (registered and signed for with a return acknowledgement slip) A lot of offices stipulate A/R (andato/ritorno) as a means of notifying someone such as the cancelling of a contract. It is the only way you can be sure that the right person gets your mail. A raccomandata now costs 5 euros plus but is the only way to know your letter will arrive. The online PO site allows you to send raccomandate without having to go to the PO itself, but allow a week to get registered and logged in. The site is only in Italian.

Having said that sending any mail out of the country works like magic – just remember to write the senders name and address on the envelope and what any parcel contains. Asking the PO for stamps now produces mild shock - it seems that stamps come very low down the list of PO priorities. It is much more important to sell you scratch'n'sniff lotto cards, insurance, and reading glasses than something to do with post and/or offices. Strange.

When I first moved to Italy I would ask people what they were doing tomorrow. 'Going to the post office' was the reply. 'And then?' ….. I soon discovered that there was no 'then'. A trip to the PO takes a day. In 2021 it might take a mere two or three hours, but still enough to make you loathe the PO and all it stands for. A glimmer of hope has arrived along with

Covid – you can now book appointments online, on the poste.it website. You just have to nominate your branch and choose a time. It will give you a QR code and time slot, and all you then have to do is turn up.

You can also use the Poste app for sending letters, parcels all manner of postal goodies. If you're a resident then you can use it for getting your SPID – a secure ID useful for being in contact with the powers that be – Tax office, social security, etc – and which will help you register on the IO app, giving you more services and general befuddlement.

CERTIFIED EMAIL

PEC – For many reasons its not a bad idea to get a PEC email address. It's peculiar to Italy, and stands for Posta Elettronica Certificata and basically means that an email sent by PEC has all the legal force of a registered letter. A PEC address is also increasingly useful for communications with public bodies, the PO, INPS and so on, and the cost is pretty risible. Probably the biggest supplier of PECs is aruba.it which cost less than 10 euros a year. There are many others such as legalmail and the PO. If you have a business or are selfemployed you should have one by now, as they are obligatory since October 2020.

Once you've chosen your address and paid your fee, you can happily start sending rude emails to ENEL, TIM and all the other providers who ignore your correspondence. Public bodies have an obligation to reply within 30 days to a registered letter or pec email, and if you get bills for something you have previously queried by pec, it stands up in court as evidence for your good intentions.

It's simple to use – when you send an email by PEC – to another PEC address, you will firstly get an email of accettazione – meaning the system has accepted it. That should be closely followed by a second email of consegna – which means its got to the right inbox. From this point on you can take the legal and moral high ground; if the comune or Vodafone doesnt read the email, it's their fault.

Cars and Driving

If you want to buy a car in Italy you must either be a resident or have a carta di soggiorno. At least for European citizens. Non EU citizens will need a permesso di soggiorno – basically you must have an address that the state can send your fines to. In practise there are sbrigapratiche who say that you can elect domicile and they can sort it. This might work for Eu citizens, for non Eu it does bring a serious risk however, as if you are stopped by the carabinieri and have your own car, without having a PdS you could be in big trouble. As most NonEu buyers just come on holiday for a month or so, they dont bother with a PdS and the anomaly in the law could be shown up in its worst light if you get caught owning a car that was impossible to buy.

The buying and selling of cars needs a substitutive notarile act – its called a bene mobile (as opposed to a house which is an immovable bene), and boats, trains, plane and cars (as well as some works of art) all need a formal 'passaggio di proprietà' so the state knows who's got what. Its not cheap, 300 euros at least but can be done by a wonderful invention called a 'sbrigapratica' or a 'hurrying along shop' which deal almost exclusively with cars and motorbikes. Even the commune can sort out your passaggio di proprietà, it's no longer necessary to sit in the notaios office for hours.

If you just want a cheap run around buy a FIAT – the older models especially run forever – anything from a 500 to a Panda to an Uno seem to be indestructible, and the spares are ridiculously cheap.

From 2019 there has been a tax on new luxury cars. Because they can. It will range from 150 (for CO2 between 110 and 120 g/km) to 3000 (over 250g/km) euros and be placed on cars and SUVs which are petrol or diesel. In compensation there are incentives of up to 6000 euros on hybrid or electric cars purchased new. For 2022, if you earn less than 30.000 euros you can buy an electric car with a 40% incentives if the car costs less than 30.000 euros. There are other incentives for purchases on cars up to 50.000 euros.

If you bring in a foreign car you can drive for 6 months on your original plates, but then you should convert the car to Italian plates, and have a 'revisione' all of which will cost around 1000 euros. The Security Law of December 2018 means that as a resident you can no longer drive a car on foreign plates and you must have it immatricolata within 60 days, or the car can be impounded. With Brexit, bringing a UK registered car into Europe from 1.1.21 means a GB sticker, and a green card. If you tow a trailer or caravan then that will need its own green card. An International Drivers Permit is not currently required for UK drivers in Europe, but as it costs 5 quid, its not a bad idea to have one in your waller for when the rules change.

From 13 Jan 2013 the European driving licence took effect. It is standard across the EU and provide for new licences every 10 years up to the age of 50 and for 5 years then on. Now Italian computers are connected to the internet it will also stop Italian residents having licences issued in other countries. So the rule is now that on expiry you must convert to an Italian licence or risk the penalties. Swansea - home of DVLC - know from October 2013 that you are not resident in the UK and refuse a renewal of your licence using a non resident address.

If you are a British national and Italian resident then you should have switched your licence to an Italian one before 31/12/20. If you didn't, then along with any other non EU resident, it's time to zip up and start learning some Italian because you now need to take an Italian driving test if it's not possible to convert your licence before it's a) expiry b) residence surpasses 2 or 4 years.

There are twenty or so countries that can still freely convert driving licences to Italian ones – the list is here: https://www.scuolaguida.it/it/Conversione-Patenti-Estere/

For newly ex EU Brits, US and Canadian citizens, Australians etc you will need to take an Italian driving test. This is in two parts – theory (in Italian and no help allowed) and a practical test.

An example of the theory test can be found here: https://www.scuolaguida.it/it/Quiz-Patente-B/ If you get more than 5 wrong, you fail. To take the practical test, you have to have a course of driving with an accredited school for at least 6 hours.

The Bollo – every year on the cars birthday it's time to pay our car tax. The car was born on the day it was matricolata – received its first licence plates – and the information is written in your log book. You will receive no reminder – and the onus is on you to go to a tabacchi which has a 'BOLLI' sign outside and pay it. You give your targa – number plate – and they tell you how much you owe. Pay late and there's interest It's calculated on your horsepower – cavalli – and always comes as a shock. There's a marvelous calculator on the tax office website which will tell you exactly how much you owe, which is thoughtful of them. You can find it at the following link:. https://www1.agenziaentrate.gov.it/servizi/bollo/calcolo/RichiestaPagamentoSemplice.htm

Scroll to the bottom of the page and choose between the calculation based on Kw or Cv (horsepower) or the second option is based on your numberplate.

From 1 Jan 2012, cars over 180 hp have a further tax of 20 euros per horse power, which is accounting for the vast amount of porsches, mazeratis and mercedes for sale at ridiculously low prices.

Car Insurance

Italy has 16 or more classes of insurance. You start, by default, at Class 14/16 – and every year without a claim you drop a class.

If you emigrate from another European country you can export your no claims discount, as long as there is no break longer than 12 months between ceasing your insurance in one country and restarting in Italy. You wont get the same discounts, but if you drop a couple of classes it makes it financially worthwhile. You will need your original insurance certificate translated into Italian which shows which class you had in your home country.

As far as companies go, shop around. The basic insurance is third party, no fire and theft and no comprehensive – the rates are too high. Depending on your commune of residence there may be minor fluctuations in price, but overall insurance costs more in Italy than most other countries.

Alternatively, you can insure via a UK company which deals in overseas insurance – Directline for instance, now operates in most European countries including Italy, but it certainly isn't the cheapest option. There were a couple of UK based companies that were much cheaper, but they have fallen by the way. With Italian policies now costing 30% more than last year, there is no way out. Shop around and gird your loins - Italian car insurance hurts.

Once you are insured make sure you always have your documents in your car, the carabinieri will want to see them all if they stop you. Keeping them on your phone is a viable option. If you don't have them, or your licence, there's an automatic fine. You should also carry a claims form in your glove box – which should be filled in if and when you have accident with both parties signing it.

Local Taxes

IMU (ex IUC, ex IMU/TASI ex IMU ex ICI)

Over the last few years Italy has run the gamut of local taxation acronyms, but none was deemed fit to stay. The latest in the list is IMU, introduced by Monti's technical government. It's now history, having gone through various incarnations, and we are at the all new IMU 2022, which is the same as IMU and TASI (2019) but all assimilated into one easier (and bigger) payment.

IUC - the imposta unificata comunale - which will encompass

the IMU, Tasi and the Tari, which are IMU and TARSU by other names. So, technically we have one tax which will cover rubbish collection, council tax and local police and fire expenditure as well as public illumination. The one little problem that they seem to have forgotten is that all the charges except the council tax (IMU) are 'imposte' and require the sending of bills. The council tax is a tax and therefore calculated by the subject and has no bill so in practise it works like this: You must calculate your IMU which but the comune will still send you refuse collection bills.

It is probable that the rates for the new tax will remain much the same as the old ones, that is non residents will pay considerably more (0.76-1%) of the catastal value, whereas residents with prima casa will have nothing to pay this year. Agricultural land was no longer be subject to IMU from 2016 , unless you live near the sea, and nor are large machines bolted to the ground.

In synthesis if you are resident in your house you will pay nothing unless you have a dependance or outbuildings, but will not have reductions on your rubbish bill. If you are not a resident you will pay IMU on everything but get a discount on your rubbish bills.

TARI

You will get a bill for this, unless you have omitted to register for the tax at the comune, in which case they will find you after a few years and send you a huge bill. The TARI is calculated on the square metrage of your home. Comunes are lazy and may either send you a letter asking if it's correct, or run off a copy of the visura and take the info as gospel. Remember that a visura is not legal proof of anything, so its a highly questionable practise, but the judicial system will side with the council on this one, so you need to bend your unbreakable spirit and righteous indignation and make sure that the measurements on your visure are accurate (at your expense obviously) and then notify the comune before they decide that your 50mq flat is, in fact, 101 mq and you have been evading tax for the last 10 years - It may be that you can detect a bitter personal experience here.

Is it worth the hassle?

For many people the idea of coming to Italy is to spend a relaxing retirement. It's certainly possible, but with the new laws on taxation it's certainly a bit more difficult that it was in the past.

For others the idea is to come to Italy and work here, or at least use their property to earn money whether the property is in their home country or here in Italy. There are those who work remotely, earning in their home country and those who earn in Italy.

This book is not a tax guide but there are a couple of golden rules to remember. Before you make the move, it's important to do your research. The double taxation agreement can and will affect the simplicity of your life, as will the loathed IVIE and IVAFE tax. The only way around this is to cut all ties with your 'home' country, which most people don't want to do.

The cardinal rule is that under the double taxation agreements, you pay tax where you earn the money. In the case of a house let, it is where the property is situated that governs where you pay the tax. You may have a house in Le Marche that you let out using a UK website, and are paid in sterling to a UK bank account but the fact that the house is in Italy means that the earnings are subject to Italian tax, not UK tax.

If you are resident in Italy, then you pay taxes here with the deductions made in your home country applicable under the RW section of your tax return. This means you will need an accountant (commercialista) in Italy who will prepare your tax returns for the June deadline. The Italian financial year runs from 1 January to 31 December, further complicating life for British tax payers who are accustomed to the UK financial April-April tax year. If you pay tax in Italy but earn in other currencies you will have to complete a quarterly INTRASTAT return (depending on how much you earn), which allows you to deduct earnings in other currencies - but you pay for the privilege.

Even if you are non-resident, your holiday home lets fall under the Italian tax system. The taxable rate is higher, but you are permitted more deductions.

If you come here as a pensioner with a UK pension you will still have to fill in an Italian tax return yearly even though you earn nothing here.

IVIE/IVAFE

These taxes were designed to stop tax evasion by Italians who were taking their money out of the country. Unfortunately the catch-all system works against foreigners who are incoming. The IVIE tax is payable on all property held abroad by an Italian resident and is calculated according to its council tax band, or its value. The IVAFE is on all investments and business held outside Italy and is currently payable on any bank account, savings account, investment or business. Fines for nondeclaration are high.

WATER – If you live in a town you will get a water bill for communal water. There is usually a lower limit to which is added your cubic metre usage over the year.

CANONE RAI - If you are resident in Italy, from 2016 you will have paid the tv licence of 100 euros along with your electricity bill from May onwards - divided into instalments. From 2017 it cost 95 euros and be divided into 6 bimonthly payments throughout the year. From 2019 it's down to 90 euros. You can only pay the licence once for your prima casa. It is not due on second homes, warehouses or garages. Nobody quite knows whether a non resident with a tv has to pay anything at all, but assume you do.. This system will probably change in the near future as Brussels has decided its not fair, and the Italian government has to come up with another wheeze.

IRPEF – Italian Income Tax. Your house has a theoretical rent, and therefore an income – so you should fill in a tax form, or rather, pay a commercialista to fill in a tax form, showing that you have nothing to pay. In practice if you are non-resident, you don't have to. However if you have taken residency to save a few bob at the atto, now its payback time. The new government is taking tax evasion seriously and the time has arrived to play by the book.

If you rent out your house, even if you declare it in the UK, tax is due in Italy as that is where the income is created.

At the moment there is a scheme to try and attract people to come and live in the south of Italy, by offering them low taxes for 5 years.   It's tempting.   How long it will last is anyone's guess but at the moment it's as follows:

If you are a pensioner who has not been resident in Italy for the five years running up to your date of application, you can now opt for a tax regime which is highly favourable.
If you get your pension paid abroad, you can now choose to pay a flat rate 7% on your income (for the first five years of your residency in Italy).

The caveats are few: your residence must be in the Mezzogiorno, ie. south of Rome, and it must be in a comune with a population of less than 20.000 people.

Bearing in mind that the Italian tax year runs January to December with tax returns due the following June, for those pensioners on a fixed income a 7% tax rate is certainly not to be dismissed. Above all any foreign property or investments which would fall under the IVIE or IVAAFE rules, will be ignored by the Italian tax man, again for 5 years.
After your five years are up you will switch back onto normal tax rules.

So, where should you think of putting down some roots? Ignore the houses for 1 euro game - if you are a pensioner you should be looking for places which are not built vertically, have access to reasonable health care within a reasonable drive, a climate which isnt too oppressive in the summer, and low year round costs as well as local shops and services. Before you sign up to buy a crumbling ruin on a near vertical mountain its worth asking yourself why the properties are so cheap. Many of the places which offer such bargains say in the blurb that they are fighting depopulation. The causes can be many, but locals probably want to live in in towns with infrastructure and access. And shops. There could be a hydrogeological risk that does not preclude your holiday home ending up around 200m further down the hill the next time you pop over for a long weekend. However the thing to remember is this. You buy a house because it is 1 euro. The buyers who come after you also want a house for 1 curo, not a house that costs 100.000 euros more. After all, you dont want to lose money on the deal, and for the buyer 100.001 euros can buy a house in the same area, nearer the sea, nearer the shops, restaurants and bars, with better access and or public transport, or art and architecture. So, while a house at 1 euro may seem a bargain, it doesnt mean you will ever be able to sell it, even breaking even. Look on the internet at the prices of ready restored properties in the area, and you'll see what I mean. Alternatively, look around more popular spots, and you will discover that most comunes in the area will have properties that are almost free, if you are prepared to spend a considerable amount of money making them habitable.

There are such schemes in Ligura, Tuscany, Sicily, Calabria, Basilicata and now Biscari in Puglia. So how far will your euro go? Well it will basically put you on a list. You will have to hand over 5000 euros in case you disappear and never do the work. You must restore the property within a set time frame and use workmen approved by the comune. You will need to make the building earthquake friendly, floors ceilings and roof. It will need a bathroom and a kitchen and probably require an electricity connection and water. You cant do the work yourself. I dont see it as a bargain.

Health Care

If you have residence and health insurance you can use the state healthcare system – the insurance company will be billed. When after 5 years you take out permanent residence status, you are eligible for free health care. The ASL will let you sign up with a doctor.

If you decide not to take residence your European Health Card will cover you for emergency treatment at the local hospital – the NHS is billed by Italy for the costs. . With Brexit, this is still valid until it's expiry. Then we are promised a new, all improved, having your cake and eating it version, but don't hold your breath. For non-Europeans its important to take your passport and certificate of health insurance to the hospital if you're conscious. Existing EHIC cards are valid until their expiry under Brexit treaties.

If you have full private insurance you will probably want to find a private hospital if anything needs doing. There are a few, in the larger towns and cities – but they are by no means numerous.

Prescriptions are expensive in Italy – and the range of medicines small. Unlike the UK where doctors can prescribe any one of over 50.000 medicines, in Italy the choice is to 6000 or so. Paying over the counter at a chemists is frighteningly expensive, but if you have any choice in the matter don't plump for the pills advertised on TV – ask for the basic version which costs 75% less.

The new laws of liberalisation of the professions mean there should be more chemists, technically one for every 3000 inhabitants, and some class 3 drugs (painkillers, cough medicines etc) will be sold in supermarkets and parafarmacie.

If you are resident with a low income (less than about 9000 euros pa) you can have the famous 'ticket' and you get all your medical care free. Normally, however, your doctor will tell you to go and get your bloods done – and you trot off to the nearest Biolab and pay 50-100 euros for all the tests. It's the same with xrays, ultrasounds, and so on – so it can work out at a very expensive business. The alternative is to walk into pronto soccorso (A&E) and fling yourself at their mercy – then it's free.

In my experience if you can find a doctor who actually does something apart from blood pressure you're doing well. They seem to serve merely as a clearing house for ill people – sending them off to other clinics and specialists – and don't want to dirty their hands with actually inspecting a patient.

Dentists. Apart from the horror stories (which are many) about Kwik Fit fitters who set up a dental practice, Italian dentists are good but hideously expensive. Many Italians go to Hungary from the north, and Malta from the south for dental care. Dentists are a bit behind the times as far as futuristic surgeries, hypnosis and a choice of whale calls for the nervous patient. You may have to go to a different place for your x-rays, and then take them back the next day to the dentist.

Alternative Medicine: Italians on the whole like to be given pills and suppositories – it makes them feel wanted. Alternative medicine has to fight against not only established cures, but against the huge hocus-pocus industry especially in the south of the country. However, you can find 'established alternatives' at an erborista.

Education

The Italian education system is laborious. You can put baby Mario into an asilo nido (nursery) almost as soon as he is born, and from there he will progress to the scuola elementare, scuola media, and then the scuola superiore which can be a liceo or an istituto. All books are bought by parents, and account for bad backs in the majority of small children. School hours are from 8am till 1 six days a week, with voluntary lessons in the afternoons. In Sicily the summer holidays start in the second week of June and schools go back in mid September. Its worth remembering if you buy a house near a school!

ASILE NIDO

They will take babies from 3 months to 3 years old, and can be private or run by the commune. Usually open from 9am to 4pm, but some of the private ones have longer hours to accommodate working parents. It's important to remember that places are not guaranteed, and you must pay – but the standard is high and the food is usually excellent!

SCUOLA MATERNA

Open for children from 3 to 5 years. Every child is entitled to go, but it isn't compulsory. There are both state and private schools.

SCUOLA ELEMENTARE

Primary School. From the age of 6, baby Mario must go to school, although he can start earlier. The dateline is 31 December so if your child is 6 in November, he can start in the same academic year.

It lasts for five years, and new legislation allows for a single teacher, which is not hugely popular – though there are separate teachers for English and maths. Other subjects on the curriculum are geography, Italian, science, music, IT and religious studies, the latter being optional.

SCUOLA MEDIA

Middle school. Children attend from 11 to 14 years and there is a national curriculum. School hours are generally in the morning, with voluntary classes in the afternoon for music, languages etc. There are term end reports – the pagella – and a written exam at the end of the third year, as well as an oral exam. Upon passing the exam the children can move onwards and upwards to the various secondary schools.

SCUOLA SUPERIORE

The secondary school system offers between 3 and 5 years of schooling – the minimum school leaving age is 16. Depending where the child goes there will be specialized education, usually after the first 2 years of general studies. The rest of your life depends on which secondary school you choose, though it is possible to switch between school in the first 2 or

3 years, if you realize that you've made a huge mistake and learning Latin wasn't such a great idea.

Secondary schools are divided into istituti – training schools which offer a vocational education and the liceo – more academically based, though all secondary school tend to follow the same national curriculum in the first two years. From the third year onwards you have to specialize.

The choices are:

Liceo Scientifico: As the name suggests the emphasis is on physics, chemistry and natural sciences, though Latin is continued as well as a modern language.

Liceo Artistico: Lots of painting, architecture, sculpture and so on, it really only leads to a university course in fine art or in training as a restorer, set designer etc.

Liceo Classico: Five years of Latin, Greek and Italian literature, plus philosophy and history of art, as well as modern languages. A sound basis for university.

Nowadays you can liceo sportivo and liceo musicale to the list.

Istituto Magistrale: Five years of study which leads to becoming a primary school teacher.

Istituto d'Arte: Three years with a diploma of 'maestro d'arte' at the end of it – more practical perhaps than a liceo artistic.

Istituti Tecnici: Five years vocational study, now with an emphasis on engineering and IT.

Istituti Professionali results in a vocational qualification in three or five years.

Once you have done your five years of secondary school you can go to university, once you have your diploma, or maturità. Famously stressful the exam is both written and oral, and has 3 parts, which are outlined on the national news in February or March, and which specify what the subjects will be for the following June.

English speaking children transferring to either scuola media or scuola elementare in Italy are usually treated very well. Sometimes a special teacher is on hand to help the child while they learn Italian, and provide extra tuition. As all teaching is rigorously in Italian, your child will learn the language much, much faster than you! In some bigger cities there are international schools, much in favour with the elite Italians as they teach the International Baccalaureate and not the 50 year old State syllabus.

Holidays

The big holidays are:

1 January – New Year's Day – very little will be open

6 January – Epiphany – La Befana – more toys for the tinies and usually the end of the Christmas school holidays. Few shops close.

Carnevale: Bigger in some towns than others, the two weeks leading up to Shrove Tuesday (Fat Tuesday – martedi grasso) see the streets full of children wearing immaculate fancy dress and throwing eggs. More of a festa for professional photographers than others, the biggest carnival is in Viareggio (Tuscany)

Easter Sunday – lamb for lunch and all day closing for the shops.

Easter Monday – Pasquetta – the first walk in the country with a barbeque for all and sundry. You will see lots of people picking wild flowers, and lots of shops won't open.

April 25th – Liberation Day – not widely observed, but most towns will have a small procession to the war memorial in the morning, and some shops will shut after lunch

May 1 – Labour Day   Much more popular than in other countries, most of Italy will be closed. Some use it for the first trip to the beach. Some shops may open and be fined by the mayor for not observing the holiday.

June 2 – Founding of the Republic – an excuse to go to the seaside, or shop.

August 10th – San Lorenzo – not an official holiday, but Italian tradition says that you go to the beach at night and watch shooting stars, though fires on the beach are no longer allowed in various parts.

August 15th – Ferragosto – the biggest holiday of the year and Italy closes except for the seaside, which will be packed to the gunnels.

November 1 – All Saints – I morti – the annual trip to the cemetery, and a good lunch into the bargain. November 2nd is an unofficial holiday.

December 8 – the Immaculate Conception – the traditional start to the Christmas season (except in Siracusa where it coincides with Santa Lucia on 13 December, and in Milan where Xmas starts on 6th December with its padronal saint Sant'Ambrogio) and Xmas lights are turned on, and trees decorated.

December 24 – not an official holiday – shops will be open till 7 and then everyone rushes home for the big meal of the Vigile di natale – and open their presents – then they go out and party.

December 25 – Christmas – bars, restaurants will be open and cinemas, nightclubs etc – Everyone goes out for a walk in the morning and after lunch – not the complete shutdown as in the UK

December 31 – Capo d'Anno – not an official holiday but the Italians love their New Year and every little town has something going on at midnight. People stay up all night and go to bed at dawn.

Add to all these the local saint – which brings a half holiday for the town, and in the cases of Sant'Agata in Catania and Santa Rosalia in Palermo bring a week of chaos. Often these local saints days are the highlights of the year and there is always something going on. San Gennaro in Naples is a great holiday for the 'miracle' of his blood, - even the pickpockets takes the day off. Firenze and Torino share Saint John the Baptist on 24 June – a excuse for a trip to the seaside, Venice has Saint Mark on 21 November, Milan Sant'Ambrosio on 6 December which makes a long weekend, and so on.

Finally the endless round of sagre and feste for local produce – there's something for everyone – strawberries, tomatoes, potatoes, cuttlefish, carrots, cheese, meat, the crowing cockerel – the list in endless, and virtually every weekend there will be a sagra in one town or other.

From 2012 all holidays, local saints days and so on, with the exception of the big state holidays (25 april, 2 June, and 15 August) were to be celebrated on the nearest Sunday, in one stroke getting rid of the long weekend, and pummeling the tourist industry, Of course, there are exceptions: Rome can have St Peter and St Paul when it likes. Milan absolutely insists that Sant'Ambrosio will continue to be on his usual day. Naples and Palermo refused to budge Gennaro and Rosalia, so after five years it's evident that it is yet another law that is completely ignored.

Earning a Living

Being self employed is the easiest option for incomers. There is still a frightening amount of bureaucracy to deal with, but the answer here is to find a good commercialista (accountant) who will deal with everything for you. Unfortunately it's not enough to open an VAT number (partita IVA) and set up shop. Qualifications are everything. Or rather, pieces of paper which have a coat of arms are everything. You only have to see an Italian degree certificate to realise that a dottore is equal to his square metre of highly embellished vellum and illuminated manuscript, which puts my typewritten A4 certificate with a tiny hologram to shame. The European Union has a directive about recognising qualifications in other member states, but acceptance of a foreign qualification depends on Italian national law, and that becomes a labyrinthine challenge.

If you have vocational training, whether it be as an osteopath, electrician or bus driver, the first steps are now enshrined in some European documentation: the European Qualifications Framework, the National Academic Recognition Information

Centres (NARIC), the European Credit Transfer System (ECTS) and Europass. To find out whether your skills and/or training are valid in Italy it's best to contact NARIC and ECTS who can tell you what your legal situation is. Nearly all professions are technically allowed to practise in Italy, but you will usually have to pass an oral Italian exam to show your proficiency in the language. Don't assume that you can learn as you go, and plan for a year without working while you concentrate on your Italian and get to grips with how things work.

The Europass system is a standardisation of documentation throughout the EU and consists mainly of a Curriculum Vitae in a standard form, a language passport, certificates and documentation and a Europass mobility document. Do all of this before you leave your home country, or you will become hugely frustrated!

With Britain's departure from the EU, the European accreditation system has vanished. Now any Brit wanting to work in Europe will not be able to use their home gained qualifications, but have to earn equivalents in Italy as any other third country. This can mean years of courses and exams to get back to where you started, unless you find yourself on the list of highly trained specialista and are welcomed with open arms.

To work legally as a self employed person you need to be registered at the CCIAA (The Chamber of Commerce). They will allow you to open a 'dita' or 'impresa' either as a sole worker, or as a company. Once you are registered at the CCIAA of your province, you are registered for INPS (the National Insurance scheme) and start paying pension contributions, whether you like it or not.

If, for example, you are thinking of teaching as a way to earn money you may be able to get by just having a partita IVA – it all depends on the contract you will be using. Teachers who work in state schools on EU funded courses, for example, are employed on a COCOPRO contract, a sort of freelancers contract. If you work for a language school, you probably will not need a partita IVA, the school will handle that side of things for you.

Jobs are rarely advertised in the local paper. You will work either because you know the person involved or have mastered the art of the 'bando'.

The Bando and the Gara – not to mention the graduatoria

Many aeons ago, to stop the system of raccomandazione (jobs for the boys) the bando system was introduced. As everyone knows, it doesn't work, but it's still there and creating more jobs for more boys. Basically it works as follows:

A job is published in the local paper, the official paper, the website. It announces what the job is and that the bando is open for a limited amount of time.   The applicant makes a written application (the gara – the competition) sending in all their documentation. They telephone everyone they know to see if their friends and acquaintances know someone on the board who can recommend them. If they're lucky a relative will be owed a favour. The bando closes and there is silence while all the pertinent information is sifted and given points. Some time afterwards the graduatoria (the scale) is published – and every candidate has points out of 100 (let's say), those with the highest points automatically getting the job. If they turn it down, the job goes to the second on the list, and so on. It means, theoretically, that a person with experience, qualifications and preferably something published should automatically get the job. However, don't be surprised that the best candidate for the job usually comes in about half way down the list.

For many incomers, the system requires years of study and application before they will even attempt a bando – the vast majority prefer to set up a little business doing what they know best – which is also, unfortunately, no guarantee of success. You may be the best osteopath in Italy, but you will need friends to make a living. Word of mouth is everything in Italy, so one local VIP as a customer is worth 20.000 leaflets left in bars. If you're planning on opening a shop or a bar, the 'new' factor is worth alot. That's the reason why bars have complete refits every 3 or 4 years. You may get a flurry at the start, but you must learn how to keep the customers after the honeymoon period, and reciprocal favours earn your place in the piazza. The business of Christmas hampers is worth a fortune – and you ignore it at your peril.

Virtually every job in Italy has a qualification or a licence attached. If you want to open a bar, you will need a licence from the comune, a certificate to show that you have done a course and passed an oral exam on handling foodstuffs, and something from the Guardia di Finanza to show that your till is legal and working. This is why people usually buy an 'attività' – an existing business - and take on an existing licence, fixtures and fittings, stock and rental contract. Staff are the only thing which don't necessarily come with the attività. It may seem ridiculously petty, but licences and whatnot were designed to stop there being 22 bars and no barber in a small town. If you have a bar the comune will tell you when you can close and take your day off – it mustn't coincide with the closing day of the other bar. And so on.

This is not to say that everyone adheres rigidly to the system. Far from it. However, as an incomer who may threaten others' trade, it's a good idea to do everything by the book, be patient and have enough money put by for an unexpected three month layoff.

If you're going to be self-employed the avenues open to you are usually on the artistic side, and here you will be positively welcomed if you're going to make jewellery, paint murals, restore furniture etc – but bear in mind that Italians are very conscious that Italian style is the best in the world, so you'll have a lot to live up to. Unless you're planning on opening a shop it's also much easier to evade the spotlight and start your business quietly, going 'legal' when it's a success.

In the last few years the government has introduced various schemes to 'simplify' your tax position. Salvini's much vaunted 'flat tax' has helped some self-employed people, but it's already being tweaked around the edges and will disappear for some VAT registered categories. Basically, at least for 2022, you can choose either a standard VAT position or a forfeit regime, whereby (as long as you dont earn more than 100.000 euros pa) you can pay a flat rate of 15% with minimal deductions on your income. The amount of deductions is all important - it ranges from around 5% to 60% of your gross, but it all depends on what your job is. Someone who sells drinks for example has a co-efficient of 40% meaning he can deduct 60% of his outgoings, while an estate agent has a co-efficient of 86% meaning only 14% of his earnings can be deducted as expenses. If you're a start up you can get a forfeit regime for 5 years at 5% which is a big pull for some foreigners keen to come and start working in Italy.

AND WHAT IF….

Making a Will:

The Italian law on succession is more complicated than that of the UK or the US. Under Italian law, a certain proportion of your property must go to family members. The calculation is complicated, but the legittima (the part of your estate reserved for the family) is laid down in the Civil Code and even if you make a will, the legittima is sacrosanct. If you die leaving only a spouse, they will have 30% of your estate. A spouse and one child reserve 50%, A spouse and two or more children – 75%. No children and your parents or grandparents get a share. A separated spouse is entitled to their legittima, a divorced spouse not.

There is no legislation in Italy for common law spouses or long term partners. Civil unions don't exist for opposite or same sex couples. To sort things out as you want them, make a will.

There are two options: you can make an Italian will leaving everything to your wife and children or you can make a simple holographic will which says that you want to leave everything under the laws of your state of citizenship. If you have a British will, your Italian holographic will simply point your Italian beni immobili towards your British will and it will be disposed of as you want.

An Italian holographic will must be handwritten, legible and be easily found in the event of your death. It's a good idea to leave a copy with your notaio or avvocato (lawyer).

Italy was a signatory to the International Wills Act of 1973, which says that as long as the will had witnesses, was drawn up by a 'lawyer' versed in the International Wills Act and is all correct, any will drawn up in another country can be valid in Italy. The problems arise with its execution. It must be translated into Italian, have a postille if necessary and will still not permit the executor to divvy up the estate, before the succession is complete.

On August 17, 2015 a new European law came into being. The UK opted out of this legislation. Before this date homeowners who were not Italian could nominate the law of their nationality to govern any will or succession. As of now, the law is clearer and yet more complicated.

Nationality or habitual residence takes precedence. HM Govt can now say that someone who has lived in Italy with no ties to the UK (for example) cannot necessarily deal with their estate under British law. It is going to take some appeals and court cases to see exactly what the UK government's position is on this issue, but it is possible that Italian property will eventually be dealt with under Italian law, notwithstanding the nationality of the deceased. In any event, it is important that in Italy you have at least a holographic will which says that you wish your estate to be dealt with under the law of your nationality, and have a proper will lodged in the UK. Wills are now easier to apply in cross border cases, once they have been translated and legalised. It is no longer essential to have an international will if you are a citizen of an EU country.

Simplified this means that if you have a holiday home in Italy it can be disposed of within the rules of your home country as long you as you have a holographic will. If you are resident in Italy then Italian law takes precedence for your Italian possessions, while your overseas possessions will fall under probate law of that country.

You can find more at https://e-justice.eu/

Death and Succession

It's an uncomfortable fact of life that people die. Even in Italy. Given the bureaucracy and strange rules, it's best to be prepared. If you find yourself in Italy without your next of kin (spouse, child, parent – in that order) its worth having a piece of paper with your instructions should the worst happen. Italian phrases for I would like my remains to be repatriated, buried, cremated etc can be googled. Especially over the last year with Covid and the difficulties with travel, there have been enormous problems in the unhappy event that a loved one drops dead in Italy. What must be remembered is that despite the law, most offices in Italy require a genuine signature on official forms, and that usually requires your presence. I had an unhappy case this year, in the middle of lockdown, where the commune would do nothing with a body until the wife arrived in Italy (impossible) or went to the Italian Consulate in London, (closed). Fortunately, the British ambassador in Rome came to the rescue and ultimately obtained permission for cremation.

It saves stress, worry and alot of time if you write a few lines detailing what you would like doing with your remains should you drop dead while in Italy. The volition of the deceased takes precedence, so if you write that you would like to be cremated/buried/fed to the fishes then it can be done simply and quickly, with the minimum of bureaucratic hurdles to jump. Obviously it would be better if your wishes are deposited with a notary or some public official – and you let your next of kin know where they are!

Burial is the norm in Italy, profitable for the Church and organised crime, but cremation is making inroads. Non denominational funeral services are virtually impossible to find in the south. If you opt for cremation you are now allowed to sprinkle ashes in some places. The church, obviously, wants them putting in a cemetery for a price at the risk of being denied entry to Paradise. However, you can now dispose of ashes on private land and at sea.

A succession – the legal process of divvying up an estate in Italy – is usually handled by a notary. It involves listing all heirs, all property, (houses, bank account, car), and calculating the taxes payable to the state for the change in ownership. Currently there are no inheritance taxes in Italy unless you are very rich. A succession should be initiated within a calendar year of the death of the interested party. If it isn't, there are heavy sanctions in place for late notification. However, these all lapse after five years.

A single or joint bank account must be frozen immediately, and this can cause problems. In the case of a joint account, it is advisable to open a new account immediately in the name of the surviving partner and move half of the balance to the new account, before handing over the death certificate and freezing the joint account. Once frozen, it is impossible to access money until the succession is complete.

In 2020 the succession became more complicated for foreigners.
When the notary does the succession, instead of just paying the taxes and fees due to the state, the Agenzia dell'Entrate will now take them directly from your bank account. This means, unfortunately, that you will have to open an account in Italy – any account will do as long as it has an IBAN. However, your physical presence is required in Italy to do this, if are you are not a resident.
If you are not British, but a citizen of another European country that signed up to the new agreement in 2016, you can help things along with a European Certificate of Succession which can be used in all member states (UK opted out of this).

Selling and Moving:

Sometimes things don't go as you planned: you may want to upsticks and go back where you came from, or you may just decide you want to move because the house you've always lusted after has come on the market. When it comes to selling, if you don't live in a big city, the chances are you should forget all the advice and experience you had in your home country.

Houses in Italy do not sell in 10 weeks, usually. The idea that you tart up your house, put it on the market, and within 3 weeks you have had a steady procession of people through the door culminating in an offer of the asking price, will remain an idea. Having said that foreigners selling are usually better at it than Italians. For a start they make sure the house is presentable, especially for the photos. They are more willing to negotiate on price after an initial honeymoon period – and don't, unlike some Italians, assume that the property hasn't sold because it's too cheap and up the price by 100.000. Foreign sellers are also more likely to have a realistic idea of the value of their house, so when an agent gives you an estimate you can talk about it like adults instead of resorting to accusation and counteraccusation that they don't understand that your house is the most beautiful, striking, wanted, sought after house in the entire country.

Most agents will still try and stick out for an exclusive agreement to sell. These can run to pages and pages of tiny tiny print – but usually say that they are for a year, automatically and tacitly renewed for a further year, and again for a third year if the agent thinks they can get away with it. If your brother decides to buy your house you will still have to pay your agent his full commission. The law which allows this practise is being tightened up. Most agents now offer only one tacit renewal, and periods of notice have been shortened, so you dont have to give three months notice on a 6 month contract. But it's not universal so read the small small print.

A non exclusive gives you the freedom to place with various agents, and sell the house yourself. The rule here is stick to the price. There is nothing that annoys an agent more than to see your house all over the internet at various prices. It does nothing for your reputation either. Some agents will reduce the price without asking you. Also, beware of overkill – putting a house with every agency in town all over the internet makes a buyer think a) you're desperate and b) theres something wrong if every agency can't sell the house.

Two or three different and varied agents with a different clientele is the best option.

Be very clear with your instructions: 'I will not accept a penny under 100.000 so don't waste my time calling me with low offers'.

Some agents try and make a bit more cash by asking you to pay for the 'for sale' sign, pay for internet advertising and so on. Refuse – remember the agent gets free advertising putting up a sign – he would much rather have a sign than not, so why pay him into the bargain.

Apply the same rules about finding a removal firm that you did when you moved out here. Don't take the lowest offer, try and get a reference or testimonial and make sure you have insurance.

As a seller you will have to pay the estate agent, and pay for the necessary certification: the CDU, certificate of conformità, and certificate of energy classification. Don't lie or pretend you don't know they are going to build a road at the end of the garden – you could be forced to buy back your house. If you sell within 5 years of purchase you could be liable for 20% capital gain on any profit you have made on the property, minus the notaios fees, and invoiced work done on the house. This can be paid at act to the notaio or, if you prefer, you can ask to pay it along with your usual tax return at the end of the year – but this is only worth doing if you pay no tax in Italy, and even then it's a questionable benefit, unless you're planning on fleeing the country to a tax haven with no tax treaty with Italy.

If you sell to a non-EU citizen then you as the seller must notify the police that you have done so, as soon as possible after the act has been signed.

Foreign sellers - some foreign sellers entrust the sale to their agent. This can create problems for buyers - not least because you won't have the sellers signature on some documents. I had an email this week from a buyer in Abruzzo who said that the owner of a property they wanted to buy was going to give a Power of attorney to the agent to sign on his behalf. This is not technically possible. As soon as an agent takes a POA he is no longer independent and is acting for the seller - so while he can have a POA he cannot ask the buyer for any commission on the sale - the vendor must pay the agent. However it must be a proper POA - done in front of a notary or the foreign equivalent, translated and legalised - and the original must be in the Italian notary's possession. Just a scribbled delega has no legal power whatsoever. The vendor can however sign a compromesso digitally - but the buyer should not hand over any money until the signed and countersigned compromesso is in his possession. It requires a clause within the preliminary saying that the deposit will be paid by traceable methods by a set time. Any bank transfer will need the CRO or equivalent trace number which will be subsequently written into the act of sale by the notary.

You should not just hand over a stack of cash to the agent, nor make a cheque payable to the agent himself, unless he is acting as the power of attorney holder.

Before you leave make sure you go to the anagrafe office at the comune and emigrate (if you're a resident). Notify the IMU,TARI and water offices.

If you sell a prima casa, then everything depends on how long you have been resident in it - up to the five year limit. If you have been resident for more than half the time you have owned it, then there is no capital gain. If less, then you will pay the 20% on any profit, minus costs.

For example if you buy a prima casa on 1 Jan 2020, take residence on 1 February and sell on 31 December 2020, you will have no plusvalenza. If however you take residence on 3 July, then you will have been resident for less than half the time you have owned the property and consequently will have to pay the capital gain.

If you sell a prima casa and do not buy another within 12 months, you may have to pay back the incentives you took at the point of sale, and lose the incentive for the rest of your life.

And that's it! Simple isn't it? I hope that in these 200 or so pages I've managed to throw a little light on the more complex issues about buying a house, and not put you off the whole idea. If there's something missing, tell me – or wait for the next update to drop in your email inbox.

To receive updates free of charge simply send a email with your name as used on your payment method in the object line, to updates@buyinginitaly.com and make sure that the address is on your allowed list. For example, if you paid via a Paypal account in the name of John Smith, write John Smith in the object field. If you bought via Amazon please forward us your email receipt as an attachment. We will not send you unsolicited mail. If you have any questions you can contact us at sales@buyinginitaly.com

Glossary - General

Abusivo	Building: built without the legal permits, Estate agent: operating without licence
Acquirente	Buyer, (compratore)
Affitare	to rent – as opposed to noleggiare to hire
Albo	register at the Chamber of Commerce with professions and their members
Agevolazione	incentives/tax breaks etc
Agriturismo	type of tourist accommodation with the proviso that the guests are served (at least in part) produce deriving from the 'farm'
Al grezzo –	rough finish – either of a building, being sold al grezzo means being structurally finished but all doors, windows, floors and plastering to do, or more specifically a particular 'rustic finish' either of plaster, wood etc.
Appartamento	flat/apartment

Archivio notarile	local archive of public acts from old notaries
Assicurazione	Insurance
Azienda Agricola	farm/farm business
Baglio	Sicilian – court yard, especially if cobbled.
Bilocale	two roomed flat with bathroom
Bolletta	Bill or invoice
Bollo	tax stamp affixed to documents. Also the yearly car tax.
Camino	fireplace
Canna fumaria	chimney
Caparra	deposit
Caparra confermatoria	deposit made at compromesso that if the seller changes his mind has to pay double the amount back
Caparra penitenziale	deposit which is returned should the sale not go ahead.
Carta d'Identita	Identity card

Carta di Soggiorno CE	permanent residence card for non EU citizens granted after 5 years of residence.
Casa colonica	farm house – large rural house
Casa popolare	council type house
Casa rurale	typical rural house usually of stone
Catastal Classification:	(click here for the link)
Catasto	the land registry
Censale	the classic man who knows a man – an illegal estate agent. Also known as a massaro
Certificato di conformità	– certificate of conformity for electrical systems, central heating systems etc.
CDU	certificato di destinazione urbanistica – a document from the local comune which explains the possible land use
Clausola condizionale	a conditional clause
Clausola sospensiva	a suspensive clause. When its conditions are fulfilled the contract is resolved

Codice Fiscale	Italian national insurance number. (click here for the form)
Comprare	to buy, also acquistare
Compravendita -	lit. buy/sell – the final act of sale but more usually the process from A-Z
Compromesso	the preliminary contract which details the sale, price, date of final act and requires a deposit.
Concessione edilizia	building concession
Condominio	a condominium – any building which has more than 3 separate dwellings with common access
Condono	a system whereby you pay a fine to put your property back on a legal footing
Conservatoria dei beni immobile	– central archive of all public acts.
Contratto libero	a rental contract for an unfurnished property which runs for 4 years, renewable for a further four.

Contratto transitorio	a rental contract for a furnished property with a maximum period of 18 months.
DDIA	a simple concession to carry out extraordinary maintenance, whereby silence gives consent – usually after 30 days.
Diritto di accesso	Right of way sometimes of only specific people
Diritto di passaggio	right of way
ENEL	the ex-state owned electricity company
Ettaro	hectare – 10.000 square metres, or 2.45 acres
Fabbricato rurale	rural building a term slowly being phased out as regards residential buildings but remaining in force for agricultural buildings.
FIAIP	The Federation of Italian Estate Agents – strictly for legal agents.
Fossa IMHOF	septic tank with run off
Grondaia	gutter

IMU	Council tax/rates/property tax– Imposta Municipale Unificata
Ipoteca	mortgage
IRPEF	Income tax (Imposta sul Reddito delle Persone Fisiche)
IRPEG	Companies tax (Imposta sul Reddito delle Persone Giuridiche)
ISTAT	National institute for statistics
IVA	VAT (Imposta sul valore aggiunto)
Manutenzione	ordinaria – works which needs no consent or permission from the commune. Usually painting, decorating
Manutenzione	straordinaria– works which need a DIA/SCIA from the commune, replacing a roof, plastering exterior walls, intonaco, any intervention in the water/waste system, electrical installations
Masseria	Sicilian usage – rural property round a courtyard, sometimes walled. In Puglia a fortified rural property.

Mc	standard abbreviation for cubic metres – metri cubi
Monolocale	studio apartment
Mq	standard abbreviation for square metres – metri quadri
Muro a secco	dry stone wall
Notaio	The notary, independent and works for the state. He is responsible for making sure the act is legal and that the buyer and the seller know what they are doing. Some notaios are better than others – having one you trust is a huge advantage. He is also responsible for taking and paying on the taxes involved with a house sale, etc.
Particella	Catastal unit of measurement – a single lot of land or building.
Persiane	Shutters
Perizia	A survey
Permesso di Soggiorno	Obligatory 'permission to stay' for non EU citizens.

Prelazione	preemption rights.
Prestito	loan
Preventivo	a written binding estimate
Prima casa	your principal home in Italy, for which you can take the 'prima casa' incentives at purchase
Procura	power of attorney
Proposta di Acquisto	written formal offer for purchase
Provvigione	estate agents' commission
Rilevamento	survey (land)
Rogito	the technical term for the final act of sale.
Sanatoria	the system to put a building on a legal footing if it were built abusively
Scaldabagno	immersion heater
Scaldino	little immersion heater for the kitchen sink etc
Scasso	channeling out walls etc for piping/tubing

SCIA	new version of a DIA
Serrande	blinds – usually as window fixtures
Soffitto a botte	barrel vaulted ceiling
Soffitto a volte	A vaulted ceiling, usually of 'canne e gesso' (bamboo and plaster)
Stima	An informed estimate
Strada Bianca	A white road – without tarmac
Strada comunale	a public road – maintained by the commune
Strada Interpoderale	a road which runs between properties and is technically public
Strada poderale	a road which runs within a property
TARI	Rubbish Tax
TASI	Smaller part of your IUC -payable in addition to IMU on 16 June and 16 December
Trattabile	negotiable

Turismo rurale	a type of rural tourism which doesn't have the same requirements as agriturismo.
Venditore	seller
Villa	large detached house. Also a catastal classification A8
Villetta	Small more modern detached house. Also catastal classification A7
Rustico	rural building or more usually in the south a skeleton of a new building, being sold unfinished

Glossary of Offices and Shops

Agenzia delle Entrate Tax, VAT, Codice Fiscale, car tax office

Brico	Usually something with Brico in the name is a type of DIY shop
Carrozziera	Body shop
Fabbro	Blacksmith
Falegnama	Carpenter
Ferramenta	Ironmonger

Gommista	Tyre shop
Idraulico	Plumber
Legname	Timber shop
Motorizzazzione	Vehicle registration authority - responsible for driving licences, car documents etc
Notaio	Office of the public notary
Sbriga pratica	High street office which takes care of car transfers, paperwork etc
Vetraio	glass cutter
Vivaio	plant nursery

Catastal Classification:

A1	Habitation 'signorile'	
A2	Civil habitation	
A3	Economic habitation	
A4	Popular habitation	
A5	Ultra popular habitation *	
A6	Rural habitation (but not a fabbricato rurale) *	
A7	Villetta	
A8	Villa	
A9	Palazzo or castle of historic or artistic importance	
A10	Office or studio	
A11	Typical house of the area such as a trullo, a mountain refuge	
B1	College, hospice, monastery, barracks etc	
B2	Hospitals and clinics	

B3	Prisons and reformatories
B4	Public offices
B5	Schools and laboratories
B6	Libraries, art galleries, museums
B7	Chapels and churches not destined for worship
B8	Underground stores & deposits
C1	Shop
C2	Deposit and store
C3	Workshops
C4	Factories and sports clubs
C5	Lidos and spas
C6	Stalls, stables, garages, etc
C7	Dutch barn type structures.
D	All to do with public/non habitable structures - note D/10
E	Agricultural

* - A6 is being eliminated and a notary will no longer stipulate an act for these types of building. A/6 must be reregistered at the Land Registy before any act can take place..

Luxury Homes:

What is a luxury home was first defined in 1969 and has subsequently been simplified or made more complicated depending on your point of view. .

The basics are these:

Villas or private parks: catastato as A/1, A/8 or A/9

If your property is 'luxury' then there is no exemption from council tax if you are a resident, and it is not possible to pay the reduced prima casa rates on purchase.

MINISTERO DELLE FINANZE

ANAGRAFE TRIBUTARIA

DOMANDA DI ATTRIBUZIONE DEL NUMERO DI CODICE FISCALE O VARIAZIONE DATI
(PERSONE FISICHE)

PARTE RISERVATA AL RICHIEDENTE

TIPO RICHIESTA

[X] ATTRIBUZIONE CODICE FISCALE
[ ] DUPLICATO DEL CERTIFICATO
[ ] DUPLICATO DEL TESSERINO PLASTIFICATO
[ ] AGGIORNAMENTO DATI ANAGRAFICI E ATTRIBUZIONE CODICE FISCALE DEFINITIVO
[ ] RICHIESTA TESSERINO PLASTIFICATO
[ ] AGGIORNAMENTO RESIDENZA
[ ] RICHIESTA CODICE FISCALE L. 27/85 N. 52 TRASCRIZIONE ATTI GIUDIZIARI ALLE CONSERVATORIE RR.II.

DATI ANAGRAFICI

- Cognome: **GILDERDALE**
- Nome: **RAMSAY**
- Comune di nascita: **LONDRA**
- Prov.: **EE**
- Data di nascita: **010866**
- Sesso: **M**

RESIDENZA ANAGRAFICA (o, se diverso, domicilio fiscale)

- Comune: **MODICA**
- Prov.: **RG**
- CAP: **97015**
- Indirizzo: **CORSO UMBERTO**
- N. civico: **160**

RESIDENZA ESTERA

- Stato: **REGNO UNITO**
- Città e indirizzo: **LONDRA, 4 CHURCH STREET, SW1 3XX**

PARTE RISERVATA AL RICHIEDENTE

[ ] ATTRIBUZIONE
[ ] ATTRIBUZIONE DIFFERITA DA S.O.
[ ] DUPLICATO CERTIFICATO
[ ] DUPLICATO TESSERINO
[ ] RICHIESTA TESSERINO
[ ] AGGIORNAMENTO
[ ] ACQUISIZIONE RESIDENZA ESTERA
[ ] RICHIESTA CODICE FISCALE L. 27/85 N. 52 TRASCRIZIONE ATTI GIUDIZIARI ALLE CONSERVATORIE RR.II.

TIMBRO UFFICIO — Il signor ha presentato modello AA4/7 — UFFICIO IMPOSTE DI _____ DATA _____

Agenzia Entrate
Direzione Provinciale di Ragusa
Ufficio Provinciale - Territorio
Servizi Catastali

Visura per soggetto
limitata ad un comune
Situazione degli atti informatizzati al 16/12/2019

Data: 16/12/2019 - Ora: 12 03.43
Visura n.: T140008 Pag: 4

Segue

5. Unità Immobiliari site nel Comune di MODICA(Codice F258) - Catasto dei Fabbricati

N.	DATI IDENTIFICATIVI				DATI DI CLASSAMENTO					ALTRE INFORMAZIONI	
	Sezione Urbana	Foglio	Particella	Sub	Zona Cens.	Micro Zona	Categoria	Classe	Consistenza	Superficie Catastale	Rendita	Indirizzo	Dati derivanti da	Dati ulteriori
1		231	1862	2	1		A/5	6	3,5 vani	Totale: 102 m² Totale escluse aree scoperte*: 102 m²	Euro 131,95	VIA CANNIZZARO n. 23 piano: T;	Variazione del 09/11/2015 - Inserimento in visura dei dati di superficie	

The Catasto

The Land Registry is a law unto itself. They should have lots of information which is freely available. Every building should be registered here, with its owner, its size, its shape and context. Given that the owner and/or professional representative can pop in and tweak their house details, it's not surprising that information is often misleading.

The three main bits of paper relevant to a property owner are: the visura, the planimetria and the mappale. Ive covered the first two elsewhere in the book, but the mappale is interesting because it's always your fault if it's wrong.

In effect the mappale is the map sheet which shows any number of buildings in a given area – (on a foglio if we're being specific). These were computerised some time ago, and often have mistakes. What will happen is this: you submit your nice new planimetria to the catasto and they won't accept it because it's different to the mappale. The outline of the house taken from the old hand drawn maps is different to the nice new planimetria. This is your fault. You cannot go further than this without getting the geometra back to check out the house and neighbours to find out what went wrong. Once he has ascertained that a neighbour's terrace was marked as a building on the original map in 1943, you must pay a few hundred euros to have the mappale changed. Then, and only then, will the new planimetria be accepted and you can inch forward in your quest to amass all the paperwork necessary for a sale.

The Catasto is going to be reformed, Mr Draghi has announced. It's been on the cards for 20 years, but it seems that this time it will actually happen. How much of a reform is still anyone's guess. Draghi has already promised that nobody will pay more, which means any tweaks will be purely administrative. What is certain is that the catastal rooms will disappear to be replaced with square metrage. This actually started in 2015, so its a mopping up process rather than something new.

Also the categories will probably disappear, so you'll have 'a house' instead of an A/3, A/4 A/7 etc. Its difficult to see how any change to the current system can be accomplished with no change in the rateable values, which are routinely upgraded if work is done to the house, but in many cases are the same as they 70 years ago. By 2026 the new system will be in force, and we are assured that even if your rateable value goes up it wont be used to calculate your IMU, which seems wishful thinking, frankly.

Residence – moving to and staying in Italy.

What follows is information for EU citizens. Non-EU citizens need to skip the next bit and read the following section.

EU citizens (excluding UK nationals from January 21)

1. No visa required

2. Foreigners are classified as tourists or residents. Full stop. A tourist is someone who is in Italy for less than three months. If you are planning on staying more than 3 months in one visit you should apply for residency

Residence

It's either/or – obtaining residence is more complex and more expensive, but leads to greater savings if you are a property owner. If you have bought a property using 'prima casa' incentives you must apply for residency within 18 months of the act of purchase, or you will have to pay back the discount you received when you bought your property.

For residence you will need:

Copies of your passport, a declaration (and proof) of income, certificate of health insurance valid for Italy, or your TEAM card, some tax stamps, perhaps a declaration of your family's status and infinite patience. If you are not the owner of a property, you will need some way of proving you live where you say you do – a rental contract, utility bills etc.

After 5 years of residence you can ask for permanent residence, now called a Carta di Soggiorno CE, for which you will have to provide a visura storica of your residence from the date you first obtained it, (fine if you have always lived in the same comune, much more difficult if you've moved about), and all the usual paperwork that by this point you will have permanently to hand.

Non-EU citizens:

A visa is required for stays over 90 days for whatever reason. Get it before you leave home.

If you are planning to obtain elective residence, ie- not work and live off your savings/pension – then you must apply for a visa for elective residency (type D), before your arrival in Italy. This is obtained from the consulate in your home country, and should be issued within 90 days of the request.

The issue of a visa is not a foregone conclusion.

To obtain a visa you will have to show title to a property and/or funds to allow your permanence in Italy – this sum is usually 3 times the minimum required for residence – so for single people around between 25000 and 34000 euro p.a., depending on where in Italy you plan to live. A couple would augment this by 20% and every child adds a further 5%. If you do not own a property, the powers that be can increase the minimum sum of funds required to account for paying rent. In addition you must have health insurance with a minimum cover of 30.000 euros.

Living in Italy with an elective residence visa precludes absolutely the possibility of working in Italy.

Arriving in Italy armed with your visa, you then go and get your Permesso di Soggiorno kit at the PO within 8 days of your arrival.

Schengen Visa:

If you are not planning to stay for more than 90 days in any 180 day period, and not intending to ask for residence in Italy, you can apply for a long term (5 year) Schengen visa, which will require the proof (at some point) of having bought a property in Italy.

Within 8 days of arrival you must complete a Declaration of Presence (Dichiarazione di Presenza) which you can do at the local police station (questura or commissariato). It applies to anyone coming from a non-Schengen country and not having one can lead to you being thrown out of Italy.

Also within 8 days of your arrival you must queue at the Poste – (Post Office) to get a Kit – (Permesso di Soggiorno Kit), which you then need to complete, queue at the tabacchi for a marca di bollo of 16 euros, queue again at the Poste to pay the bollettino and fees, and then queue again to submit your completed kit. Start learning Italian because you will be required to show you know some. After 6 years it can be converted into a long term Permesso, and you will have to pass an Italian language test to B1 level.

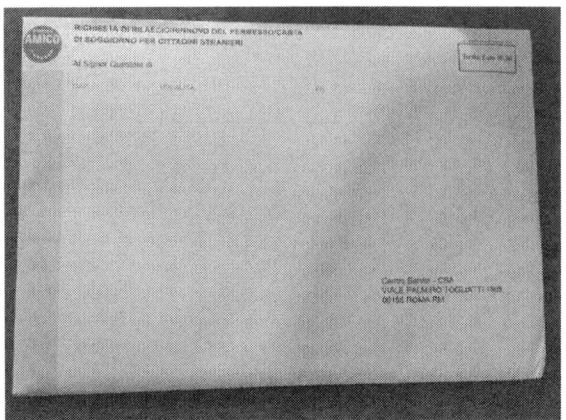

Permesso di Soggiorno

There are many and various types, though the function is the same – and it is important that the reason for your stay is the same as that granted on your visa. You can apply for the PdS at a larger Post Office, and it usually takes up to three months to be issued. You need the yellow kit which will also require:

1. The completed application form plus the payment made

2. A passport plus photocopies of both the photo page and the visa page

3. 4 passport photos

4. A tax stamp (marca di bollo)

5. All the documentation relevant to the type of PdS you are applying for.

When you take your completed kit back to the PO, you will get a receipt for the kit, once checked over and a date for your an appointment at the Questura, which could be for months hence. At this appointment you will have your photo and fingerprints taken, and a receipt given. At some point after that you will receive your electronic version of the Permesso di Soggiorno. It will have to be renewed every year for the first 5 years – and you must ask for the renewal at least 60 days before its expiry, so it is quite likely you will have to renew it before you have received it.

After six years of being a model non-citizen you can get a PdS for 'long stays' and not have to go through the rigmarole annually. You will have to take a language test. After a further five years you can apply for citizenship.

Types of Permesso di Soggiorno

Per coesione familiar (family cohesion) – which is issued for the spouse and children of an Italian citizen

    Details of family, marriage and birth certificates

Per Lavoro (work) – a work permit for employees

A declaration from the employer and other documentation especially if a seasonal worker

Per Lavoro autonomo (self employed)

Adequate resources to carry out your business, a certificate of inscription at the CCIAA in the relevant register, proof that there are no reasons to stop you from carrying out your business (licences etc), somewhere to live, and proof of an annual wage not inferior to the minimum required for free health care. Add to this a VAT number (partita IVA)

Per turismo (tourism) which is for anyone staying for more than a week in a non official structure such as a hotel, registered B&B, etc

Proof of health insurance and independent financial resources

Per Studio (study) – a students permit

Proof of health insurance and a letter of acceptance from the school or university etc

Per Ricongiungimento familiare – for the family and dependents of a person married to an Italian citizen

Details of family, marriage and birth certificates as well as special 'nulla osta'

Per Dimora – those who are planning to live here but don't intend to work. – also known as elective residency.

1. Visa issued by foreign Consulate.
2. Copy of the documentation to show the necessary economic resources (pension, investments, etc), and title to property.
3. Copy of insurance policy for health cover for the period of your stay in Italy or a copy of the adherence to the Assicurazione Volontaria (state health insurance system), with a copy of the payment made, as well as a copy of the formal request at the Health Office.
4. The payment slip (bollettino postale) for the smart card (30,46 euro) and another for the payment of a Permesso di Soggiorno (40 euros for 1 year or 50 euros for 2 years, if eligible)

Some of the documents may need official translations and it's best, certainly in Sicily, to arrange this before you arrive in Italy.

Here's a link which shows you how to fill in your PdS application:
https://www.unive.it/pag/fileadmin/user_upload/ateneo/internazionale/documenti/destinazione_cafoscari/soggiorno/stay_permit_kit_instructions_RENEWAL.pdf

Obviously first timers would tick the RILASCIO box and not the RINNOVO box.

Once you've got your PdS you need to renew it at least one month before it expires. Make lots of copies and keep the original in a safe place or you have to start all over again if you lose it.

Already Resident …. GB only….

If you had your residency in Italy before 31.12.20, then you are advised to get the new Carta di Soggiorno elettronico to help you negotiate the Schengen borders. There is a paper version available from your comune, but the powers that be have decided that it must be in English and standardised.

For this reason the Italian government is now issuing this new card. It is valid for 5 years. If you already have permanent residence in Italy – (ie have been resident for more than five years) then it will have a validity for 10 years.

You will need to make an appointment with your local questura for the application – most questuras now have a dedicated email address to contact them for the appointment. You will need to take with you the following:

> A currently valid document (ID) – carta d'identita, driving licence

> Proof of your inscription at the anagrafe of your comune that shows you were resident on 31.12.20 or an autocertification your inscription by this date, and

that is wasn't subsequently cancelled (artt 46.47 of the DPR 445/2000)

Receipt of payment of 30.46 euros, made by bollettino postale on CC 67422402 to: MEF DIP.TO DEL TESORO VERS: DOVUTO RILASCIO CARTA DI SOGGIORNO with the causale: "Importo per il rilascio della carta di soggiorno - Accordo di recesso UE/ UK")

4 passport photos.

Habitual Residence

There are quite alot of questions about what constitutes Habitual Residence. In Italy it exists, on paper.
Now most countries decide that habitual residence is where you have the centre of your life and family, even if you don't spend half the year there.   In Italy it's a much more open question. Tax residence, as we know, is more than 183 days a year.   Could the powers that be decide you are habitually resident if you spend less than that time in the country? Assuming you have no other home in another country and spend your time gadflying from one friends sofa to another, it's possible.   For most people this won't happen. In fact, if you study all the references to residenza abituale on Italian websites they only deal with the question of IMU.   Here the taxman could make a killing.   If you are resident at one address, lets say a spacious villa with a rateable value of 1000 euros but are habitually resident in a pokey 1 bed flat with a rateable value of 200 euros, then the tax man will come after you for the missing IMU payments on your spacious villa,

which you wont be paying as your residence is currently exempt. For foreigners who have second homes in Italy, and presumably are not resident, then there is no possibility that the taxman can claim you have habitual residence. The grey area is for those who have an elective residency visa, to stay in Italy more than 90 days at a time, and are residents in a particular comune. If 'they' decide that you are habitually resident in Italy, then you could be forced to pay Italian income tax on your worldwide income, even though the whole point of having an elective residency visa is to avoid this possibility. Whether it would hold up in court is another matter. To be honest, it's not even worth worrying about.

Notaio's costs.

The following calculations are based on these hypotheses:

- A single sale in a single comune, the property of a single owner

- Visure catastale and ipotecarie which take a certain amount of time and resources

- Four copies of an eight page act

- The consideration of legal, fiscal and planning problems

- The act taking place in the notaio's studio and not being stipulated elsewhere.

The minimums and maximums are not absolute but serve to give a guide for the purchaser.

Price of the Property	Euro	Minimum fee	Maximum fee
Price up to	93,000	1681.30	2428.80
Price up to	139,500	1805.50	2617.40
Price up to	186,000	1933.15	2830.15
Price up to	232,400	2029.75	2991.15
Price up to	280,000	2157.40	3203.90
Price up to	370,000	2254.00	3364.90
Price up to	465,000	2478.25	3738.65

To be added to this are the registration, the taxes and IVA (VAT) at 22%. For example an act of sale of a first house for a price of 150.000 euros would be:

Fees paid by the purchaser	
Registration Tax and duties	3000
Stamp duty	250
Archive tax	50
Ipoteca and catastal tax	50
Visura ipotecaria	130
TOTAL	3,480

NOTAIOS COSTS	From 1,933.15	To 2,830.15
IVA at 20%	From: 386.63	To 566.18
TOTAL	From 7,624.78	To 8,701.33

To the Notaios costs should be added the costs incurred for other visure, VAT and other costs not otherwise written

The Purchaser can also ask for the calculations to be done on the catastal value of the property x 115.5 in the case of Prima Casa and x 126 in other cases – independently of the price paid at Act- and given the large difference in the south of Italy, everyone does this! Also, in this case the notaio reduces his fee by 20%.

Purchase with a mortgage granted on the property.

If the mortgage and the act of sale are stipulated at the same time, it is normal for the notaio to grant a reduction of the notarile fees a line with the guidelines of the district.

To add to the following figures are the taxes and fees for the registration, and public administration (in particular the notarile archive and the Tax Office), and VAT (IVA) at 20% on the fees.

Bank mortgage of a duration of more than 18 months

Mortgage value – up to (euro)	Minimum fee	Maximum fee
93.000	1,349.00	1,721.60
139,500	1,413.40	1,818.20
186,000	1,500.80	1,949.30

232,400	1,602.00	2,082.70
280,000	1,684.80	2,206.90
370,000,	1,749.20	2,303.50
465,000	1,901.00	2,531.20
695,000	2,048.20	2,752.00
930,000	2,324.20	3,145.30
1,162,000	2,453.00	3,338.50

The taxes and fees are usually a percentage of the amount lent. For example for a mortgage of 300.000 euros the fees and taxes are:

Fees and charges undertaken by the client:	
Archive tax	24.10
Fees for the 'Conservatoria' and the Catasto	35.00
Visure ipotecarie	130.00
TOTAL	189.10

Notaio's fee	From 1,749.20	To 2,303.50
IVA 20%	From 349.84	To 460.70
TOTAL:	From 2,228.14	To 2,953.30

Add to this taxes on the mortgage which range from 0.25% for a prima casa to 2% for a seconda casa.

Architects' fees

The work of an architect is split by law into the following phases.

A   Base project

B   Preparation of a summary estimate and of the technical report

C   The executive project (drawn to scale)

D   Specialised estimate (computometrico)

E   Execution of construction and decorative detail

F   Assistance in the hiring and contracting, and sourcing materials

G   Direction of works, with periodic site visits (in the necessary number), organisation and actuation of all works projected in their various phases and supervision of the same to a finished and satisfactory end.

H   Responsibility for the execution of works and assistance to the client for successive phases of works up to a satisfactory conclusion.

I   Carrying out of contracts and works, accounts and such up to and including the execution of the finished works.

Once determined for the above points, payment will be fixed as a percentage of the cost of works, the ten points of which are subdivided by law with regard to the services of an architect.

The ten points are shown in Table B and are as follows:

A	Base project:	0.10
B	General estimate	0.02
C	Executive project	0.25
D	Specialised estimate	0.10
E	Construction and Decorative details	0.15
F	Hiring and contracts	0.03
G	Direction of works	0.25
H	Assistance at collaudo	0.03
I	Termination of Works	0.07

These sums are as a percentage of the overall cost of works. For example a restoration of 100.000 euros, would have A as 1000 euros, B as 200 euros C as 2500 euros, and so on.

At the point of payment, as determined above, IVA will be added in accordance with the law at a rate of 2% of the overall payment. (or 20% of the architects fee)

Guide to IMU /Tasi/Tares

In 2022 the IMU will incorporate TASI as it did in 2020 - and it seems that the calculations will remain the same, though we are promised a new unified tax imminently, which will be easier to calculate.

Luxury Homes: for those with a luxury home IMU will be payable on a prima casa at a maximum of 1% and with only one deduction of 200 euros permitted, and no deduction for children living at home. Tasi will also be payable up to the maximum of 0.33% as above, but the combined value cannot be more than 1.14%

Second Homes: All other buildings and homes will pay both IMU and TASI, with a maximum combined rate of 11.4 per thousand - ie 1.14%

Rented property: Between 10 and 30% of the TASI must be paid by the renter, a choice dependent on the comune. The IMU is paid entirely by the landlord. If the property is leased and not rented all the TASI is at the charge of the renter.

The following is how you calculate IMU using an online calculator

PRIMA CASA: *IMU is not payable on prima casa, unless it results as A1, A8 or A9 at the catasto in which case there is no exemption.*

Using an online calculator such as this: http://www.calcolaimu.it you will be presented with various options:

SECOND HOMES: for those of you who do NOT have residence in Italy or at the address for which you are liable for IMU the calculation allows for no detractions, and the aliquota will be different. For communes which have not yet set their aliquota - (it can range from 0.46 to 1.06%) the default is 0.76%.

The payment must be made in 2 tranches: the first on 16 June, and the second by 16 December.

SPECIFICS:

If the property is prima casa for one person and seconda casa for another, then the rates are calculated accordingly.

You can no longer have two prima case in the same commune - ie one in the name of the husband and one in the name of the wife. The main house is where the nuclear family (and children) reside - so children can no longer have houses in their names in the same commune.

If you are divorced or legally separated there are further restrictions on payments, basically that the IMU is at the charge of the partner who has been assigned the property, and not necessarily the owner. If there are two properties in the same commune, only one can claim prima casa. In two separate cities, each can claim the lower rate. Only one of the properties can claim the child discount.

If you have two garages/box auto - you can only claim one as a pertinence to your prima casa - if they are catastato apart from the main residence. The same goes for cantine, soffitte and tettoie if they are not catastato within the main residence.

If you have two buildings but which are both the same house and they are catasto in a single unita Immobiliare - you will pay at the prima casa rate. If they are catasto'd separately then you choose one as prima casa.

In a villa bifamiliare - it is not possible to do a catastamento unitario as they are 2 distinct dwellings and therefore prima casa can be paid on only one of the dwellings.

If you have a second house in which your child lives - it remains a second home and there is no discount.

If you rent a property, you are not subject to IMU .- it is the landlord who must pay.

PAYMENT - The new simplified F24 is the form to use: Get it here:

http://www.agenziaentrate.gov.it/wps/wcm/connect/d093ba804b686f0faf8fafdc987dc2b1/F24+semplificato_mod.pdf?MO

D=AJPERES&CACHEID=d093ba804b686f0faf8fafdc987dc2b1

It is in two sections - both are identical - complete both and one will be returned by the bank as your receipt.

In the first section complete the payers details - this is pretty self-explanatory

In the section 'Motivo per pagamento' it should contain - in the Sezione column the destination of the money. There are three options: ER for erario, RG for region or EL for ente locale. The latter will be the one to use for IMU for most prime case. The grey fields are for those who use the form for IMU and mean:

In the space: 'codice ente' - you put the catastal code of the commune - a letter and 3 numbers

In 'ravv' you put a cross if the payment is contested for a previous year (leave it blank)

In 'immob variati' you put a cross if you are presenting a declaration of variation (leave it blank)

In 'acc' put a cross if you are paying in two or three tranches

In 'saldo' put a cross if you are paying all in a single solution

In 'numero immobili' put the number of buildings you are paying for

In 'anno di riferimento' put the year in 4 figures. So for this year it will be 2019. If you have also crossed the RAV box then you can pay for the contested year (in arrears)

In 'detrazione' you put the total amount of deduction you are entitled to.

In 'Importo a debito versati' you put the amount you are paying - so net of detractions to the nearest euro - round up if 50 cents or more, down if 49 cents or less.

For some tributes such as Erariale there is a minimum of 12 euros. This is not applicable to IMU unless the commune explicitly gives an exemption, so for a bill of 8 euros you should pay in two rates of 4 euros each.

RATEAZIONE/Mese rif

0101 if you are paying the whole lot in one go.

0102 if you are paying the first of 2 tranches.

TRIBUTE CODES - The tribute codes must be right. But everyone ignores the 'state' share. For the prima casa payers its fine - it all goes to the commune.

- 3912 principal home and pertinences (Comune)

- 3914 land (Comune)

- 3916 buildable area (Comune)

- 3918 other buildings (Comune) (2nd homes)

-3913 fabbricati rurali for agricultural use (Comune) - only valid for registered farmers.

The TASI code is usually 3961

Bonus 2022

Most bonuses (tax credits) have been prorogued for a further year. These are applicable for residents who are tax resident in Italy and file a tax return. For 2022 the detractions and incentives are as follows:

Bonus Facciata: Up to 60% for the repairing of facades in a centro storico for 2022, with emphasis on insulation and energy efficiency, though repairing balconies etc is also included.

Bonus Restoration: 50% for work of restoration up to a spend of 96000 euros, both for single residences and condominiums, IVA included for ordinary maintenance.

Bonus Furniture: 50% deductible for a maximum spend of 10.000 euros only if the purchase comes after works of restoration.

Ecobonus for Energy Saving at 65% - this changes this year:
boiler bonus: 65% deductible if you install a Class A condensation boiler with contemporaneous installation of individual thermostats on radiators
50% if you install a condensation boiler Class A
0% if you install a boiler Class B
Cedolare secca 10% on controlled rents.

New 'green' bonus - For terraces, balconies and condominiums you can offset 36% on costs up to 5000 euros.

To get these incentives the paperwork is detailed and payments must be made by bank transfer with specific wording. One mistake and you lose the lot. Banks may help, but usually your geometra or ingegnere can help with making sure the paperwork is submitted correctly. If you do your own tax return it will be even more difficult - but the savings justify using an accountant to get the full allowance. Most of these credits are spread over 10 years.

SISMA Bonus 2021
This bonus allows a detraction for antiseismic works of restoration on houses and factories/laboratories. It is valid till 31 December 2021

You can use the incentives for either a prima casa or a non resident house in zones 1,2 and 3 and the bonuses amount to 50, 70, or 85% of the works carried out.

Earthquake bonus: anyone who does work to reduce the seismic risk of a building in zones 1-3, and reduces the risk by a single class can claim 70% of the works back. If you reduce the risk by 2 classes the incentive rises to 80%.

In a condominum works will gain an incentive of 75% if there is a reduction of 1 class, and 85% if there is a reduction of 2 classes.

The works must be carried out between 1 Jan 2017 and 31 December 2021. They must lead to a reduction of at least one class of risk. The works must be carried out on 1st or 2nd homes, condomiums or buildings of production. The buildings must be in zones 1,2 or 3 according to the classification of 20 March 2003.

The maximum spend is 96000 euros, IVA included. It can be deducted over 5 years. This limit also includes the amount spent on the classification and verification of the seismic risk.

A list of Italian comunes and their risk classification can be found here:
http://www.buyinginitaly.com/wp-content/uploads/2018/01/all_1_Com_Class.xls
It's an excel file.

110% Ecobonus for 2022/2023

Unsurprisingly lots of people are very interested in these new incentives. What makes them different to all the other current incentives is that its not a credit on your tax bill over 5/10 years, but actual cash. This makes it all the more appealing to non resident/non taxpayers. Be warned, however, that it's a long and complicated process trying to qualify. As a non taxpayer you have only two options – cede the credit to a bank or financial institution/person, or get the building company to take on the debt and write it off over 5 years on their tax liability. There are very few builders who are capable of taking on such debt, so to cede the credit to the bank you will need 36 different pieces of paper, and unless you are fluent in Italian and with a good understanding of how the bureaucracy works, it not something to take on lightly.

The incentives are not available for everything – in fact the criteria are strict. First and foremost, any work you do must increase the energy efficiency of your property by two classes, and its based on replacement and not new systems. So to get a new energy efficient boiler you must already have an old inefficient one in the house. Same with airconditioning. What you can add new is photovoltaics or solar panels – if they are allowed where you live.

You can also use the incentives (up to a limit) for insulation/coinbentazione within certain guidelines – it must, for example, cover at least 25% of your vertical and/or horizontal external surfaces.

Any work done must increase the APE class of your property by 2 classes – easy enough if you have a class F or G house, but virtually impossible if you are Class C or above. But a little wriggle room allows you to include a colonnina for recharging your electric car into the bargain which may make the difference. Obviously there is an upper limit to any work done, but you can use it for either a condominium (all the owners must be party) or a single dwelling. It is available for prima and second homes.

What you will need is a competent and prepared geometra/engineer/architect who is prepared to deal with the paperwork. Not all of them are, as the legal responsibility they bear is total and the extra insurance they need will put alot of them off.

At the moment the incentives are valid until December 2023 but the percentage is likely to be 90% instead of the current 110%. I have had many phone calls from people who assume the grants will cover the entire cost of tarting up a house. They won't. If you are contemplating popping over to buy a house, complete the purchase and apply for the incentives before the cut off date, you can forget it, frankly.

In addition there are bonus' and incentives to buy electric/hybrid cars, electric bikes, furniture, white goods, spectacles. For some of these you need to be a low income bracket, for others you need to pay a fair bit of income tax. Most are inconsequential for non resident/non taxpayers.

EMERGENCY NUMBERS

The Europe wide emergency number is 112 and is valid in Italy – though is primarily for the Carabinieri.

Other specific numbers in Italy are: 113 – police, 115 – the fire brigade, 118 – ambulance, 117 – the guardia di finanza, 1515 – fire alarm for woods and forests, 1530 – emergency at sea.

Links

Useful sites for anyone who needs to know more!

http://rome.angloinfo.com - visas, Permesso and Carta di Soggiorno

http://www.esteri.it/visti/home_eng.asp - visas – US, Canada, Australia, New Zealand, South Africa

http://poste.it/azienda/ufficipostali/eli2/soggiorno/guida/eli_soggiorno_inglese.pdf - Guide to the PdS kits

House hunting portals:

www.immobiliare.it

www.casa.it

www.cercacasa.it

www.idealista.it

www.vivastreet.it

Forums:

www.italymagazine.com

www.britishexpats.com

www.italy.forumotion.com

Printed in Great Britain
by Amazon